The slow suicide...

I was intending for this story to be the final chapter of my second book, I can't imagine that anything is going to even compare as far as stories go, at least not in the time of this writing, and it just didn't seem to fit into the "book of short stories" I was contracted to compile.

So, if you are looking for the book of mildly comedic short stories (my bread and butter) that you were promised almost a year ago, you may be disappointed.

This just seemed more important at the time, that time being "this" time.

Don't worry, there is still comedy in this story. Even a massive stroke, however down-played it was on my social media for the sake of my family, could not kill my sense of humor.

Good times leading to better times...

It all started by making friends with a musician/comedian/author I had become a fan of by way of a much more famous comedian's podcast that I listen to every Tuesday morning while doing pool service work.

Though, our meeting and becoming friends had nothing to do with my ever trusty, if a little battered, body turning on me in every way possible. He gets to share this story by way of proximity to the events.

I met Mishka Shubaly after a show he played here in Phoenix about a year and a half ago. I had seen him play several times before this meeting, and I had talked to him several times in Facebook messenger while I was extremely drunk and dealing with the reality of my estranged daughter coming to live with us. But up to this point, I had not met the man face to face.

I'm not one of "those fans," those fans who try to occupy a performer's time after a show. I buy merch,

I tell them I enjoyed the show, then I fuck off back to where I came from.

But this was different, we had been engaging in an ongoing conversation over the course of several months. He was aware of who I was, he was aware of the situation with my daughter, and he really seemed to care.

I took my daughter to the show, she loved it, and at the merch table, the star of the show greeted me as if we really knew each other. I have no idea if Mishka knew how much this meant to my daughter, a girl just getting to know her father, but it really did. In her mind, I knew a famous musician, even though we were seeing the show in a Phoenix backyard converted into a stage complete with downtown dwelling Phoenix bums sitting right next to us.

My friendship with Mishka continued over the next year and a half through text messages and the occasional visit to the southwest to play a show, always giving my wife and me the VIP treatment at his shows. Then, the next morning coming over to the house so I could make sure his road weary Toyota van was going to make it to the next stop. I'm sure some of Mishka's professional comedian friends or musician friends would look sideways at me, working on Mishka's van. I'm sure that puts me squarely in the category of a "mark" a "shill," but I don't mind, Mishka talked to me regularly before he knew I could do anything for him. Working on his van was no different than working on Claude's motorcycle for free. This was a friend of mine, and I have a gift for understanding and repairing mechanical things that I no longer have any interest in exploiting for financial gain. Also, and more importantly, I love spending time in my shop with friends.

This year for my wife's and my anniversary, he used his friendship with the aforementioned "famous comedian and podcaster" to get us into a very private, exclusive party being hosted at the comedian's house located in both Mel's and my favorite little town in southern Arizona.

To say it was a party, wasn't doing it justice. First, we got to watch a movie that wasn't scheduled to be out for months, written and starring another fairly well-known comedian and co-starring a who's-who of stand-ups. Not only that, the comedian in question, the writer and star of the movie, was sitting three feet away from us in a room the size of my garage while we watched.

After the movie, the room that was permanently set up as a bar, complete with actual bar, TVs above the bar, and bar stools, that had been temporarily converted into a make-shift movie theater, was then converted into a comedy club.

The host, as I have said, is a very famous comedian. I'm not naming names other than Mishka in this story because I don't want to go through all the trouble of getting permission. By "trouble," I really don't want to bother any of these people with my silly bullshit stories, and if you are a fan of stand-up comedy, then you already know who they are anyway.

As I was saying, the makeshift movie theater was then converted into a makeshift comedy club. Our host, one of our favorite standup comedians, was not performing. He had just shot a special for the now defunct "Seeso" streaming service just a month or so ago, and currently didn't have an act, after burning all of his material for the special. But his lack of participation, did not even come close to disappointing. I don't know why or how, but two incredible, headlining comics were going to perform for free, from three feet away in a 20'x20' room.

I had heard of the female comedian, but neither Mel or I had seen her act. Two jokes in, we were both immediate fans.

The male comedian was someone the two of us were already huge fans of, first seeing him on comedy central years ago for the roast of Charlie Sheen, and then seeing everything he has done since.

Both absolutely killed. This was not a comedy show, this was a comedy experience straight out of our dreams. We were in a tiny room packed with maybe thirty people, seeing headlining comics at the top of their game, and drinking for free.

*Author's note: We were drinking for free and gladly accepted the drinks we were offered. But, I never show up to any party without paying some sort of tribute by way of giving alcohol to the house. So, we showed up with and offered up a fifth of Tito's vodka and an 18-pack of PBR. That's just good manners.

After the show in the tiny bar on the host's property, he moved the crowd outside to an outdoor stage where an up-and-coming female music/comedy duo, whose music had been recently closing out his podcasts, were setting up to play for the party.

And play they did, belting out lullabies for drunkards and trailer-trash, while chugging tequila, making out with each other, and simulating sex acts between songs. It wasn't a spectacle for the sake of being a spectacle, mind you, it was part of their act. It was all perfectly choreographed to lead into the next song, or to close out the last, and their songs were far better written and performed than any song about "washing your big ol' pussy" really needed to be.

As the cops showed up to let the group know that the show was over, it was clear that the party was just beginning, though we would not be there for it.

Mel had fallen asleep on a piece of lawn furniture. I will give her credit, she lasted longer than she usually does after this much sustained drinking, and she really was trying to fight the good fight. But, as the war on sleep goes, she had not won the war, she has never even won one battle. So, after thanking our host, we quickly left the walled compound, trying to make as little noise as possible up the quiet small-town Arizona street, that my Harley could manage.

For fans of stand-up comedy, this was a perfect night. Melissa and I will never forget it, and we will always be grateful to Mishka for making it happen.

A descent into embarrassment...

Several months later, my life was as good as it ever had been. I had released my first published work as a writer, and it was doing far better than I had realistically thought it was going to do. It was not a commercial success by any means, I was not going to get to meet Oprah, I was not going to get to see my name as an author in the New York Times, there was not going to be some imaginary dump truck full of money backing up to my door... But, I was published. You could read something I had written on actual paper, and for 24 hours my parents could see my work sitting at number 9 in the bestseller list on Amazon. On top of it all, I was getting paid decently well for my efforts.

I was still working my pool service gig. I was still working as a welder out of my shop. I had no reason not to, as both pay me well, while allowing me the freedom of my time being my own. And, I was getting extra money from something I really loved, while people kept giving me unbelievable compliments, buying me drinks, and giving me drugs.

The icing on the cake was that Mishka had invited me on a trip with him back to that small Arizona town to hang out, while he played a show there to kick off him playing a week of shows in Phoenix as part of the "Bird City Comedy Festival."

As this trip was getting closer, I was contacted by the co-host of the famous comedian's podcast. He had read my book and was thinking of being the voice on the audio of the book, and considering I was going to be in town with Mishka, it would be a perfect time to talk about it.

I picked up Mishka at Phoenix Sky Harbor airport in the early afternoon. Mishka looked visibly relieved to see me pulling up to the arrivals gate in a full-sized Chevy pickup truck, and not my motorcycle. He even remarked that he had never seen me driving or traveling with anything but the Harley and was really happy to see that we would be traveling the three hours south, in relative air-conditioned comfort.

The drive was fun, lots of storytelling from both of us, and I was really enjoying it. Most road trips I go on, the only talking happens when we stop for gas, the bathroom, or a beer.

Don't get me wrong. A motorcycle is by far the superior mode of travel. The inability to talk to anyone but yourself leads to endless existential examination and self-examination that just can't be compared to any other form of transportation.

But, I had a professional storyteller trapped in a rolling metal cage with nothing to do except tell me all the background stories that made up the many questions I had thought about, the many times I had seen his act. And all the better, it didn't have to be annoying, we had nothing else to do except look out at the endless miles of desert through a windshield.

As I have said, I had been hitting it pretty hard for the last few months, and the long, sober drive was painfully working my nervous system.

To be honest, for weeks, all those telltale warning signs that I had been going way too hard for way too long had been doing their job, warning me, but I, like most alcoholics, was ignoring them.

When we got to Mishka's friend's house, the place I would be staying, I was offered a cocktail, and boy I needed it. The second large and strong vodka drink in less than 30 minutes was probably just a bit more than I needed.

Forty-five minutes after arriving in Bisbee, AZ, I was drunk, and having more drinks with the cast of my favorite podcast, in the very spot that they record from. The bartender from said podcast was making me drinks, the co-host was offering to get me stoned. The famous comedian was on tour, so would not be in attendance, but after two years of listening to everyone else in the room, all podcast regulars, I had become every bit as much a fan of them as I am the comedian. I was living every fan's dream. Drinks, jokes, and stories with the people who had entertained me, through so many hot days full of hard work, far out in the Arizona desert.

But, like many star-struck fans often do when faced with the reality of being temporarily let into the inner sanctum of their comedic heroes, I drank way too much, and to top it off, the co-host had offered me weed.

To explain, I love weed, but it doesn't like me very much unless weed and I are at home alone, and there is no alcohol involved.

Earlier in the evening, when I was first offered the herb, I declined while explaining all of this. Three or four vodka drinks later I was asking if I could hit the pipe. I knew as I was hitting it, it was going to fuck me up, but the night was almost over and in my drunken mind, I just couldn't pass up the chance to smoke with Co-host. I kept thinking, "You may never get this chance again," well that's the kind of drunken thinking that leads to never getting that kind of chance again.

The weed did exactly what it always does, it sent me straight over the edge. As soon as I smoked it, I also did the second thing dumb fans do. They (me) forget that I listen to them every week, their stories and jokes are a part of my weekly life, my stories and jokes are not part of theirs.

They don't know my punchlines like the boys at the bar do, so when you are so drunk and stoned that you forget the punchline, after telling your best joke wrong... you look like an asshole.

More on that later.

I don't remember leaving, I don't remember going to sleep at Mishka's friend's house. My next memory was being in extreme pain and puking in a strange bathroom.

As any of my drinking companions can attest to, I'm not a puker. I can count on one hand the times I have thrown up from alcohol in my life, and still have at least two fingers to flip the toilet off with. But I was puking. Not only was I puking, but I was in blinding pain in my lower back and couldn't piss.

I must have been making a hell of a racket as this was going on, because I could hear someone moving around and I was sure that it was really early in the morning. I couldn't have told you why I knew it was early, in all of the pain and confusion, but I knew it was.

I stumbled out of the bathroom and looked around and started to get a sense of where I was. I found Mishka's friend out on the patio smoking a cigarette and apologized for the mess I just made, but that I needed to go to the emergency room. I had this pain before, long ago in my early twenties, I was passing a kidney stone.

Mishka's friend was far better than anyone could hope for in a host, he took me to the emergency room and helped me check in. I have always prided myself on being a good guest, the embarrassment at destroying his bathroom and having him take me to the hospital haunts me to this day. I hope to make it up to him, but I am not sure how I could. Hallmark doesn't have a card for, "I puked everywhere and then screamed in pain in your car," I know, I checked.

The Bisbee, AZ emergency room was very much like every emergency room I have recently visited in one way, they instantly calculated that I was a junkie. I would have liked to have said something along the lines of, "No, madam, I am not a junkie, but just your run of the mill working class alcoholic." But in the face of searing, mind-numbing pain, my wit had left me and I found myself answering their questions in the most pitiful way possible, ass hanging out of the hospital gown, hanging on to the bed railing as if my very life depended on it.

I have never faulted junkies for much. I have known many of them over the years and for the most part, I just feel sorry for them. They went looking for heaven and found out hell is a real place, and we build it ourselves.

But, my sympathy ends when I must wait an hour at an emergency room for relief in the form of morphine because junkies have been trying to pull the "kidney stone scam" for as long as there has been emergency rooms and junkies.

Now, because of this, if you are legitimately in pain, you have to wait until the lab can confirm the presence of a stone by way of a CT scan.

An hour later, the nurse came into my room and gave me a mixture of morphine and tramadol. I had passed their test and my prize was pain free blackness...

My next clear memory was Mishka sitting next to my hospital bed, a look of concern on his face. I can't clearly recall what was said, a sign that the pain meds were doing their job. Something about texting him when I knew how long I was going to be, something about whether or not I had talked to my wife, etc....

I hadn't, she had no idea that any of this was going on, and she wouldn't until she got off work. My wife is a very dedicated school teacher and leaves her phone off while teaching class, she checks her phone a few times during the day, but I didn't want to text her during her lunch break and have her worrying about me when there really wasn't anything she could do about it anyway.

I don't remember Mishka leaving the hospital room. He was there, then, just more comforting blackness.

My next memory was of the doctor waking me up to tell me I was going to be discharged. He gave me a stern lecture about drinking in that way that any "so-called" authority figure who finds the very idea of having to talk to the likes of me, does. I had already asked him earlier in the day if last night's drinking had caused the stone, he had said it hadn't.

This lecture wasn't about my health, he had proven several times throughout the day that my well-being was not his primary concern.

His primary concern, to be very clear, was that I had no insurance and I looked very much like a deadbeat to him.

His second priority seemed to be making sure that I knew how much of a waste of time I was for him and his staff.

My health was a distant third, if at all.

In all the excitement of drifting in and out of consciousness, screaming agony, throwing up, and pissing blood, I had somehow managed to break my right index fingertip in the hospital bed railing. And not wanting to interrupt his carefully crafted, self-righteous lecture about the evils of alcohol abuse and what he erroneously believed to be my financial situation, I never even bothered to mention it to him.

I was booted to the streets of Bisbee with the bill, and the advice that I should drink lots of water and that I can safely eat 8 over-the-counter ibuprofens within a 24-hour time period.

Mishka dropped me off at his friend's house with my truck so I could convalesce for a little longer before he played a show here in Bisbee.

A few hours later, I suffered my second kick to the balls, this one completely my own making.

I received a text from Mishka letting me know that he would be picking me up soon to take me to the Funhouse where I had been hanging out the night before with Co-host and the crew, and that Mishka would be getting ready for the show. The following text said, "Also, no soft way to put this: you gotta be on your best behavior tonight, both at the Funhouse and at ****'s. Shit got a little too loose last night."

Fuck! I didn't know what I had done. The last thing I remember was smoking a bowl with Co-host, and the next memory was waking up in pain and with a bladder full of blood.

The entire wait for Mishka to pick me up was spent trying to figure out what I had said or done while kicking myself for kooking out in the midst of my heroes.

OK, in the spirit of full discloser, it wasn't the only thing I was doing, I was pacing back and forth holding my kidney. The stone had ripped a bloody path of destruction from my kidney to my dick, leaving me in the kind of pain that causes the strongest among us to sweat, shake, and vomit.

Any thoughts of not showing up at the show were now gone with one text, I had done something I needed to make up for, and I needed to be there to do it, mind numbing pain or not.

On the ride back to the Funhouse, Mishka told me what I had done, I had said something along the lines of, "I believe that white people should be able to subjugate the other races," not only had I said that, I had said it in front of Co-host's mixed-race kids.

Now before I start to try to defend the indefensible, this is the opening line of a joke I tell. Some (very few) reading this, have heard the joke. The joke kills if you know me, or possibly if you don't, but if you like fairly tasteless off-color jokes, and of course, if I actually finish the joke. But I didn't. Instead, I started the joke, didn't fill in the premise, and left out the punchline in a room full of professional comedians.

If you thought that the indignities and unbelievable pain of a kidney stone, a day in a hospital full of hospital workers, who were completely convinced that I was a drug addicted scumbag, would compare to how I felt as Mishka explained what I had said... well let's just say that I would have traded ten kidney stones and ten cunty doctors for a chance to go back in time, undrink my last two cocktails, and unsmoke that bowl.

But, as we all know, once a thing is said, it can't be unsaid. There is no Planned Parenthood for words.

Back at the Funhouse, I had taken on the demeanor of a dog who had just pissed on the carpet. But to everyone's, who was there, credit, I wasn't treated that way.

The morphine had completely worn off and I was in real pain again while everyone was getting ready for the show. I asked ****, the Funhouse bartender, for a beer and sat outside to smoke and work on controlling the pain when Mishka walked up and told me that he was leaving to start setting up for the show, and told me to catch a ride with the Ch****'s.

Instead, I tapped Co-host on the shoulder and asked him, even though it was him and his family that I had offended in the most egregious way the night before.

This may seem counterintuitive on many levels. First, everyone there was more than willing to give me a ride. I was Mishka's friend, and everyone there, no matter what indiscretion I had committed, stand by their own, even little hangers-on like me, just a friend of a friend.

But, Co-host isn't just one of theirs, he is one of mine. He is the kind of guy who can replace his own head gasket in his truck, fix his own leaking roof, and feed a fool his teeth if that fool was needing a teeth meal.

And as much as I am for mixing with people outside one's social tribe, Co-host was as close to my "tribe" as I was going to get. And with the amount of pain I was in, and the amount of shame I was feeling, I needed to be around the only person there I felt like I related to, even if his response was to break my nose...

I tapped him on the shoulder, I told him the situation, and his reply was genuine, "Yes, you can ride with us, no problem."

On the ride to the show, Co-host and his wife treated me like the same way they had treated me from the first time they met me, like long lost family. In pain, sickly, acted like an asshole, you would never have known it. The next person who trespasses against me is in luck all because of these two.

The show in Bisbee was great, Kristine Levine and Mishka killed as well as a few lesser-known comics. I tried my best to hold it together during the show, but the pain was winning. The aftermath of the kidney stone was doing its work, and to make things worse, to get to the bathroom, you had to cross the stage. Every time I had to piss blood or puke from the pain, I had to interrupt someone's act. Finally, I gave up and started puking and pissing in the alley, the idea of going to jail for public urination, being preferable to interrupting a comic's work.

I didn't make it to the afterparty. I asked Mishka to drop me off at his friend's place so I could get some rest. Lying down felt so good, not pain free, but with every step I had taken all night, my kidney shot fire and rusty razorblades into my back.

In the dim light of the open bedroom door, I noticed that my broken finger had turned white, and that I hadn't noticed any pain from it since I left the hospital. I rubbed it with my other hand and felt nothing, it was completely numb. I touched it to my face and it was dead-cold.

I couldn't even think about it at this point. My brain was shutting down. If I moved, my kidney hurt, if I thought about my day, my brain hurt. I just had nothing left to worry about, whatever was going on with my finger, and I let exhaustion take me.

My kidney felt considerably better in the morning. It still hurt to walk, but I was functional and obviously healing up.

My finger, on the other hand (so to speak), decided that it wanted to take over for my kidney. It was still numb to the touch, but deep inside near the bone, it was radiating pain in waves.

I'm a skateboarder of 33 years, I know the pain from broken bones, even the pain from broken fingers, this was not that pain.

The only way I can describe it is when you freeze your fingers then run them under warm water. That pain of the nerves coming back to life. Except, that pain ends when the blood warms up, but this pain never stopped.

I tried to not think about it and was thankful for how comfortable my truck was as we drove back to Phoenix.

Mishka had a weekend full of shows to perform for the "Bird City Comedy Festival," so I had him drop me off at home and let him take my truck as my only plans for the weekend were to get more rest, and to see his and Kristine Levine's show Saturday night with my wife. If I was not capable of riding my motorcycle, we could always take Mel's car.

Back at home, my system started to settle down and I started to realize that I was constipated. I'm not used to doing drugs like morphine, it's been years since I dabbled in opiates, but now I was facing their lesser talked about, uncomfortable side effects. I asked Mel to get me some laxatives, and by morning, I was starting to feel better.

I spent all day Saturday lying on the couch holding heat on my finger. It was still white, it still seemed like the blood wasn't flowing to it, and unless I kept it warm, it hurt like hell. My kidney felt fine now, but my stomach was acting up, giving weird pains and really bad gas that I chalked up to ending the constipation, and the fact that I was eating 8 ibuprofens at a time to control the pain in my finger.

That night Mel and I rode the bike downtown to see Mishka Shubaly vs. Kristine Levine perform for the second time in two days (for me), but this time I wasn't puking, I wasn't pissing blood, and only had some minor pain in my finger and in my guts. I can tell you that their show was good while pissing blood and in blinding pain. But, it was way better while I could actually enjoy it.

I also have to mention that as we showed up, Mishka handed Mel a shirt and ushered us into the show with the performers. I have gotten to get into shows for free, I have gotten to see the inner workings of a live show before the audience is seated, the conversations about sound, the excitement as performers go through their rituals, the empty hall, the echo of footsteps as the audience starts to file in and take their seats, but Mel hasn't, and I really thank both Mishka and Kristine for letting Mel experience that.

Sunday, it was clear something was going horribly wrong with my intestinal tract. I had a pain in the high left side of my guts that was getting worse by the hour. But, it was still manageable by kidney stone standards, so I did what I have always done, and ignored it. My finger was still in pain, but it was starting to look a little better as the color was starting to come back and I didn't need to keep it hot all the time, just most of the time.

Mishka returned my truck with the plan being that I would drop him off at the airport for his return flight back to the east coast. We exchanged signed copies of our books, this beautifully written hard cover, with a beautifully written personal message to me in the cover of his book. He received a puny little paperback full of my silly bullshit and typos, and an equally silly message scratched in mine.

My five-day weekend full of embarrassment, pain, and missteps was officially complete.

That night Mel made me go to the doctor. My second trip in four days. I had diverticulitis brought on by constipation due to morphine use. Four days ago, I was pissing blood, and now I was shitting blood. I was really starting to think that I was not living right. I don't believe in magic, I don't believe in karma, but this was getting a bit ridiculous.

I wasn't sure if it was the antibiotics or the fact that I was being forced into sobriety for the first time in a couple of years, but I was getting depressed. It didn't help that my finger started to turn black and the skin was starting to fall off.

I was five days into the diverticulitis diagnosis when we once again made a trip to a medical professional, this time to an urgent care. All of the other trips had been to real doctors, but I don't have insurance, and this shit was really starting to add up, so we went to the place poor people go, urgent care.

The physicians-assistant who saw me was a nice guy. He tried his best prescribing meds for pain, antibiotics for the obvious infection, and splinted the finger.

For the next few weeks, I laid low. I took a break from booze, and I didn't do any drugs. My finger was fucked, but the diverticulitis cleared up and I generally felt pretty good.

Mexico will fix it, right?

Things were settling down a bit health wise. My finger still hurt, but it seemed to be getting better, however slowly. I was getting back to my routine of riding, drinking, and writing. The book was still doing well and I was riding the wave of adulation from strangers and friends alike. I was sure I was past this little physical "hiccup," and I was ready to move on. So, like any sane person, I took a motorcycle trip to Mexico.

This time this trip was not just fun and games. We were there for a reason and that reason was that a friend had bought a RV back in the States and was having it moved to Puerto Peñasco, Mexico to a lovely spot on the beach on the Sea of Cortez.

Yes, we were going to party, but during the day we would be working on his used RV making sure everything worked, troubleshooting the things that didn't, and getting a lay of the land before his family started using the RV in a few weeks.

I would like to say the ride to Puerto Peñasco was uneventful, and honestly, it usually is. But not this time. The police in the small border town of Sonoyta, Mexico have bills to pay and they had a plan for paying them. They had set up a speed trap about ½ mile from the border, and if you looked like you had money, you were speeding.

I learned a few things as we paid the cops off. First, I learned that my Spanish sucks. I mean it really sucks. I thought I was having a conversation about my vacation and I was really being interrogated about whether or not I was drinking and driving. I had the money to cover the drunk-driving bribe, but once I figured what was really going on, I quickly changed my tune and was very forward telling the cop I had not been drinking (I had been) and doing my best to change the subject to our friend who was the reason we were being pulled over, having long hair.

This leads to the second thing I learned. The Mexican code of machismo! You see, our friend hauling the RV is Mexican. Let me rephrase that, he is of Mexican descent. Our friend is really about as Mexican as I am. He grew up in Phoenix riding the same skateboards, drinking the same beer, doing the same drugs, listening to the same music, and fucking the same chicks that every other American skateboarder who grew up in the United States in the 80's and 90's did.

If he had a race, it was the same as mine, that race being skateboarder. But, the Mexican cops did not see it that way.

You see, our friend was one of those Americanized Mexicans, complete with long hair and shorts, and long hair and shorts are just not something a "real man" does in the eyes of "real" Mexican men.

So, there I was, throwing my friend under the bus to the Mexican cops, but his bribe was paid, and if I could avoid paying another by making fun of his hair to this cop... Well fuck yes, I was going to do it!

We partied the same way we always do in Mexico. We drank heavily, there may have been some drug use, we got kicked out of one of the premier resorts in Puerto Peñasco (a story for another time), but this time it left me exhausted. I feel tired every time I go to Mexico, but not like this, I didn't even feel like riding my bike back, all I wanted to do was sleep.

Great, I'm going to bleed to death from my dick...

Monday, back at home, I had to go back to work. Everything had been going so well for me recently, financially speaking, that I could have taken the day off, but taking days off was not how this newly found financial freedom had been built.

So, tired and hungover from three days in Mexico, I forced myself into the garage to finish grinding the parts I had fabricated for a local environmental cleanup company who I occasionally do welding and fabrication work for, and wait for their representative to show up to pick the parts up and drop off a check.

I have been a welder/fabricator at a professional level for almost 20 years. You would think that all that experience would lead to me being just about as safe as anyone could be. I have seen more than anyone's fair share of some truly horrible work-related accidents after all. But, I'm your average working man and I cut corners. We all do it, every hard-working man who has a dangerous job working with tools and equipment made to shred wood, melt steel, or break concrete, does it every day.

They cut corners on whatever little piece of safety equipment gives them a rash, or makes them hot, adds extra time to the job, or in some way fucks with their workday. So, they forgo said safety equipment and they roll the dice. Most of the time everything is fine, most of the time...

For this part I was building, I had to weld on little steel bars that help to hold everything in place as I build the part. The last thing I do to complete the build is to take a cut-off wheel and cut these steel bars off and store them for the next build.

You may know nothing about welding and fabrication, but take my word for it, a cut-off wheel is the second most dangerous tool you can use. First off, they are very sharp, they are made to cut steel after all. Secondly, they are fragile. They are a very thin disk made of fiberglass, resin, and carbon metal shavings. Finally, they are spinning at incredible speeds. The grinders I use in conjunction with the cut-off wheels turn at 12,000 rotations per minute and have more torque than your mom's Honda Civic.

I made several safety mistakes that morning. I didn't feel like wearing pants, I was fresh off my morning swim and didn't even have underwear on, just swimming trunks.

But, my biggest mistake was not examining my grinder and cut-off wheel.

As I said, cut-off wheels are very fragile, very thin, and they are prone to damage which is why you always do a visual inspection of your wheel.

Well, I didn't.

I fired up the grinder and started cutting with a wheel that had a crack in it. I don't know how it got cracked, I probably set the grinder down after I used it the last time in a rough fashion, or it was a manufacturer defect, it really doesn't matter.

I didn't check the wheel, and when I started cutting, the wheel exploded in all directions, the most important direction being my crotch…

If you have never accidently cut yourself, I mean really cut yourself so that blood is pouring out onto the floor, there is no pain, it doesn't hurt like a paper cut, instead, your brain goes into "save your life mode."

As the first drops of blood start to hit the floor, you are dead calm. You start to apply pressure to the wound through your clothes and start looking for anything that can be a bandage before you even look at the wound.

I found a fairly clean long-sleeved t-shirt hanging on the back of my office chair and calmly took my shorts down to find a small, maybe ¼ inch cut in the main vein running down the length of my dick, you know the one, the main one.

Instantly, the shirt was soaked in blood, when I removed the shirt for a second look, blood shot out four feet in front of me.

I don't really know how to describe how it felt to see a four-foot spurt of blood shoot out of the shaft of my cock... Bad? Yes, very bad. Surreal, panic inducing... I was faced with the idea that my wife or son were going to find me dead from blood loss, curled up on the shop floor holding my dick.

I have made many jokes over the years about being found dead with my dick in my hand, but the reality of it was just not as funny as I have often portrayed late at night at the bar.

I was just starting to get lightheaded when the bleeding stopped.

I had moved to the master bathroom, dropping blood all over the house as I walked, to get a look at how bad it was under better light and contemplate the idea of calling 911, when I saw that I was no longer leaving blood on the floor.

I took my dick out and looked. The tiniest little remnant of a cut was there on the shaft. If not for the blood in my shorts, you would scarcely know anything had happened at all.

I sat there on the toilet with my pants down for several minutes while I collected myself and finally cleaned myself up.

I should have dialed 911...

An hour and a half later I was at a steel warehouse with my friend, Nome, waiting for our steel order to be cut and loaded onto my truck. We were talking about motorcycles, or past glory with motorcycles, something motorcycles related. I pulled a cigarette from the pack, placed it to my lips, lit it, and the whole world turned sideways.

I had a numb, tingling feeling that started at the top of my head and headed down my chest to my left arm, and I started seeing double.

The cigarette fell from my lips onto the ground as I fell to one knee, grabbing on to Nome to keep me from falling over I said, "I think I'm having a heart attack."

I quickly recovered, and Nome started to help calm me down. He knew I had spent the weekend partying in Mexico and has even been in Mexico partying with me a time or two. He has seen me have a cocaine induced panic attack in the past, he has seen me believing I was going to die, and thinking that was what was going on, he calmed me down.

I felt fine for the next couple of days, fine for me anyway, I'm always feeling some kind of pain. That's the nature of life when you work hard and play hard in your 40's after a lifetime of working hard and playing hard.

Wednesday, I had an average day. I went to work doing pool service around 6am. After work, I had a nap, and when I woke up from my nap, I went to work in the shop on a welding job.

During the welding job, I drank four beers (I know how many because it was the last four beers in the fridge), made a late dinner, then went to bed around 1:30am. It is a completely average time for me to go to bed when I have multiple jobs going.

At 4am my alarm went off. Everything seemed fine during my morning piss, but then I wasn't really thinking about it.

As I made my way up the hall from the master bedroom to the pantry to retrieve coffee filters, it felt as if the hall was tilting side to side as I tried to walk. I opened the pantry door and I couldn't remember why I was there and closed it without getting a coffee filter. I walked to the coffee pot, put the pot under the faucet and ran the water, added coffee without the filter, never put the water in the coffee maker, and left the full pot of water in the sink.

This entire time, the room kept pitching side to side as if my kitchen was suddenly on a boat in rough seas.

I stopped the coffee making process completely and held on to the countertop to keep from falling over as the room tilted and buckled around me. I closed my eyes and thought, "Damn, I must not have slept good last night, fuck it, go back to bed."

I walked sideways holding the wall all the way back to the bedroom and I set my alarm for an hour later and fell back to sleep.

At 5am, my alarm went off for the second time and I shot out of bed. I don't have to punch a clock, there is no boss that is going to yell at me for being late. I'm fighting the heat of the Arizona sun and waking up an hour later means being in the sun an hour later.

I walked out to the pantry, grabbed a coffee filter, cleaned up the mess I made on my first attempt, and headed out to my office to read the news and smoke a cigarette.

After a few cigarettes and a couple of cups of coffee, I felt almost normal, just running later than I wanted to be.

Mel was up at this time and we started talking while I got dressed for work.

She had seen that I had gone back to bed and I started to explain what happened, but as I did, the words came out in a jumbled mess.

It took four tries for me to explain that I thought I must have not gotten enough sleep, and we both laughed about how funny it was that I couldn't talk and believed that I just needed more coffee.

I left for work and drove to the gas station to get my morning coffee, cigarettes, and iced tea. Except, my speech had not gotten any better. I felt perfectly awake and alert, I just could not talk. As I fucked up what I was going to say to the girl at the gas station, she compensated. I have been stopping at this spot for the last five years and I don't even think she noticed I was having trouble talking, she was on auto-pilot as most of us are at that time of the morning.

For the most part, I don't talk to anyone during my work day. Most of the pools I service either the homeowner is out of town, sleeping, or just doesn't want to be talking to service people.

I'm fine with that, I don't want to talk to anyone either, I want to put my earbuds in, listen to a podcast, and try to get "in and out" as fast as humanly possible.

I don't get paid by the hour. The faster I go, the more money I make, and nothing adds more unpaid time to your day like talking to some rich asshole who doesn't understand that wind carries leaves into a pool.

On my Thursday route, I do have a couple of exceptions: Kathy, who is as cool as a customer gets, so cool that she has become close friends with both my wife and me. A person that I changed my entire route around so that I can spend time hanging out with her and her dogs because, fuck it, if I can't spend time around Kathy, what's the point of working for yourself.

Every Thursday, Kathy, the dogs, and I hang out after I do the little work I have to do to maintain her two fountains. After the work is done, we stand around her kitchen counter and gossip, tell jokes, and occasionally she will have me answer the phone to fuck with her employees.

Why does Kathy have me answer the phone for important business calls? Because it's funny. Her employees know by this time that she is having her pool guy answer the phone. We have been doing it for almost six years now, but it cracks her up every time.

They are scrambling for her time, trying to make her money, make themselves more money with her money, and the pool guy is now dictating whether or not they get to talk to her.

For the first time in six years, I was dreading going to Kathy's house. All morning while working, I had been practicing how to talk, how to put together sentences, and I was failing. My ability to talk was getting worse, and with every failed attempt to speak properly, I was getting more and more frustrated and worried.

I managed to explain, in very broken speech, that I must have not gotten a very good night's sleep. Kathy knows that I spend a lot of time working late at night to help supplement my income and she was completely understanding, and very worried about me.

My next stop where I would have to talk was at my good friend Priest's house, he was out of town, so I was able to slip in and out without having to talk.

By this time, I was realizing that trying to talk was causing me a bit of discomfort. It wasn't pain, but it was physical discomfort. It was kind of like the feeling you get when you are about to sneeze, but you don't, except that feeling lasted as long as I tried to talk.

I finished my route for the day and headed home. I was getting hungry, normally I stop at Chipotle at the end of my Thursday workday, but I realized I wouldn't be able to order, so I got take-out from Ammaccapane's bar near my house. I knew Cheryl works Thursdays, not only does she know my take-out order by heart, Cheryl isn't really listening when she makes conversation.

Cheryl tells you about her day, then asks questions about yours, but she isn't really listening to the answers. It's all just white noise to her as she thinks about what she is going to say next, and in my current situation, this formula was perfect.

I got home, sat down in front of the TV, started eating, and started googling my symptoms on my phone.

This is when I realized that it wasn't just my speech that was affected. Trying to type was working every bit as bad as I was speaking. It struck me that my ability to think was completely fine, but my ability to communicate was completely fucked.

Finally, after several attempts, I was able to type "I can't speak" into the search field and Google did its thing...

It didn't take much reading to put a name to my symptoms, and that name was "aphasia."

This entire time I had been telling myself that I must have not slept well, hoping it was the case, that I would take a nap, and everything was going to go back to normal. But, what I found in the Google search results let me know that "normal" wasn't something that was going to happen anytime soon, if ever again.

There are two causes of aphasia: a stroke or a brain tumor.

I didn't even finish my lunch.

Mel was still at work for the day and she normally can't read or respond to text messages, but today I got just a little bit of luck. I texted, "Emergency, need hospital, at home, can't talk…"

And she responded, "I'm on my way."

She got home within minutes, the school she works at being only two miles away. I showed her the Google results, she could hear the problem in my attempts to speak, so we filed into her car and off to the emergency room we went.

The stress of being at the hospital made the aphasia worse.

By the time the receptionist was asking questions, I wasn't even able to say my name. Fortunately, Mel and I have been together for 23 years and we know each other so well that we don't have to talk. She can voice a paragraph from me just by the look on my face and she took over being my voice.

The nice thing about being in the emergency room for an actual emergency is that you get to cut the line. There is no waiting on paperwork and no sitting down. As soon as the receptionist heard my symptoms, the doors to emergency room proper swung open and two very large men in hospital scrubs sat me down in a wheelchair. One started wheeling me in, while the other helped me remove my shirt and began to affix a heart monitor to my chest.

Both men helped me into a bed, and before they even completed the task, I was bombarded by two doctors and a nurse asking me questions, taking blood, checking my blood pressure, listening to my heart, and asking more questions.

The main question they kept asking was what drugs I was on. I kept telling them that I had not been on any drugs since Saturday, but the cardiologist, a tall good-looking man who smelled like old money, was having none of it. He was convinced that I was a methamphetamine addict and that I had to be lying to him.

I was scared out of my mind. I had just been told that I had suffered a stroke and that I was way past the timeframe that they could use the "clot busting" drugs that would have saved some severe and permanent damage, and now all I could think of was wiping the smug look off this cunt's face as he called me a liar.

"A-a-a-as said-d," I said with my newly acquired speech impediment, "d-did did did..small of c-c-cocaine-aine on Saturday.. do some couple of times year... no speed... hate speed... o-o-o-only occasional dr-dr-drug use... check blood!!!"

This seemed to satisfy everyone except the cardiologist who left the room with a self-righteous look on his face.

I met with a hematologist who took more blood than I thought possible, but at least he seemed to be a nice guy and didn't seem to assume what had caused my problem. Later, I found out that he didn't assume because he was the one tasked with finding out a verifiable reason for my stroke, and in true scientific fashion, he reserved all judgement and went about the task of doing the actual science. More on that later.

Next, I was rushed into the cath lab for a CT scan of my head and arteries in my neck. That scan found nothing, but that was good news (kinda). That meant that they could not see any bleeding in my brain, but it also meant that more invasive tests would be in order.

I was fitted for a hospital gown, you all know what they are, from here on out my ass would be hanging out in the most literal sense, and I was moved upstairs to the regular hospital for an indefinite stay.

Though highlights and highly entertaining things were very rare in all of this, the nurse who took me up to the main part of the hospital from the emergency room and got me set up in my new room, was one.

Now we have all seen the trope, the Hollywood stereotypical "take no shit" black nurse: quick with an insult, quick with a joke, not about to put up with your shit, invoking Jesus every third sentence...

Well, she is a real person and she was currently working at a hospital in north Phoenix.

By this time, I had been in the emergency room for about three hours and Mel needed to leave and pick our son up from school soon and the emergency room nurse was turning me over to "Black Nurse"(I really wish I could remember her name, but it had been a very long and frightening day).

Mel waited around for me to be moved and settled in my new digs, and I was sure glad she did. If not, people, including myself, may have thought I made Black Nurse up.

Black Nurse made it clear from the first second that she wasn't about to put up with any shit. As she entered the room, before addressing me in any way, she was yelling at one of the emergency room nurses about how her shift was ending soon and how it was bullshit that he couldn't accomplish this simple task, the task of moving me. I instantly liked her.

She wheeled a wheelchair up near my bed and motioned for me to get in. I must have not moved fast enough because she yelled at me, "Get in, I know you can walk."

Over the next 10 minutes, from the emergency room to me being safely in my bed with a TV remote in one hand and nurse station call button in the other, I received one of the longest and most heartfelt lectures I ever had in my life.

It started in the elevator when she asked me when I first noticed the stroke symptoms. I told her what had happened, how I had gone to work, trying to talk to the cat after work, the entire story. Her reply was, "Typical man. Too dumb to take care of yourself."

This was followed up by a rant of epic proportions. She ripped me a whole new ass about my alcohol and drug abuse, working too much, not taking care of myself, how I was cheating my family by all of these actions, etc....

She finished up by giving me a hug, a real hug. Then, looked me in the eyes and said, "I'm off for four days, I will be thinking of you and praying for you."

She was the last person I encountered while in the hospital that talked to me like a person and not a job to be done. A stereotype of a black nurse caring for a stereotype of a white-boy biker.

Mel returned from picking up our son from school and the waiting game began. It was now 9pm and I had not seen a doctor since being moved from the emergency room. The nurse in charge of the floor came in to check on me and I complained about being hungry. The nurse told us that they were no longer serving food for the night, but Mel could go out and get me food and that there were several fast-food places nearby.

If I had known that it was going to be the last time I was going to get to eat for the next two days, I would have asked her to go someplace better than Jack in the Box, but it seemed like everything was going to be fine, that I was just going to spend a night in the hospital, and I would be home soon.

After dinner, I told Mel to go home. I was sure that they were not going to do anything more to me that night. I was sure the kids were worried, and I was exhausted.

A hospital is not a restful place. They tell every one of your loved ones that you need your rest, and then the hospital staff makes damn sure you never get any.

First off, even though I had shown several times that the stroke had not affected my motor function, I had been listed as a "fall risk." A "fall risk" meant that they were worried that I would fall out bed, fall walking to the bathroom, etc.....

When you are labeled a "fall risk," they take special precautions like setting an alarm on your bed that lets the nursing staff know if you have left the bed for any reason.

I understand the reasoning behind this for many people in my condition, but I had already been tested in every way possible, regarding mobility and motor function. I had been in the hospital for over twelve hours by this time and had been going to the bathroom by myself the entire time, so imagine my surprise at an ear-piercing alarm going off. Then, three nurses and a doctor rushing into my room at 1am while I was trying to quietly walk to the bathroom to take a piss.

The floor nurse was pissed at me, "You have to tell us if you need to use the bathroom."

I was equally pissed, but I had lost the ability to vocalize it. I wanted to say, "How the fuck am I supposed to know that, and why the fuck is the alarm on the bed anyway?"

What I managed to say was, "Why? W-w-w-why?"

Her response was, "Because you are a fall risk."

I managed, "No n-n-no, not!"

If you have ever tried to plead your case to a temporary authority figure, you know how frustrating it can be. If you have ever tried to plead your case to a temporary authority figure while having a pronounced stutter and the inability to form complete sentences... Well, let's just say it's next to impossible.

Secondly, the vampires come at exactly 3am.

I don't know what they were doing with all that blood, I have never seen any "follow-up" blood tests charted in my medical records, but every morning a very jovial, overweight gentleman in hospital scrubs took at least six vials of blood at 3am.

This would not have been so noticeable if they had used one of the two IV's that were stuck in me, but this guy had to stick a new vein every time while trying to talk to me about absolutely nothing.

It was obvious he had no idea what I was in there for, it was also obvious that he was just doing what the doctors had ordered while being a really nice guy, but it was 3am, I was tired, and I couldn't talk, so I just stared at him blankly night after night.

Mel returned that morning around 8am, just in time to hear that I would not be allowed to eat until an occupational therapist showed up to perform a "swallow test." The problem with that was no occupational therapist was scheduled, nor would there be one, until the doctor in charge ordered it.

It was a long, boring morning for Mel and me. It was 11am and none of my doctors had come to see me yet. We spent the morning doing something we never do, watch TV. We don't have cable TV. Shit, we don't even have over the air TV. We stream everything over the internet, so for us, there is no channel flipping, there are no shows that we didn't find from a recommendation or something we hadn't been waiting years for.

TV had not changed much in the years since we stopped letting program directors and networks decide what we watched, but we did get to see the show "Impractical Jokers." Probably the best hidden camera show I have ever seen, and we got to watch hours and hours of "That 70's Show," a forgotten favorite.

Around 2pm, two orderlies came to the room and moved me and my bed down two floors to radiology. I received a CT scan, then an MRI. I was still unable to talk, so the men did their work while I lay there silently.

Several hours later I was visited by a neurologist carrying the results of the CT and MRI. With a smile on his face and an upbeat demeanor, he told me that I had had a stroke. He showed me where the stroke had happened and proceeded to tell me that my prognosis was not very good. He was very confident I would, at the very least, have a pronounced speech impediment, but most likely I would never be able to talk or write properly again.
I wasn't mad at him, I wasn't mad at the situation, I was mad at the suggestion that I couldn't beat this thing. I was one day in the hospital and my speech had already gotten a lot better. I was practicing with Mel and by myself, alone in my hospital room.

This diagnosis was not going to work for me. Who the fuck was this guy, he didn't know me.
He didn't know all of the times I had pulled off the impossible. He didn't know how many times I thought I was dead and I pulled my shit together and beat the odds.

All I managed was, "B-b-b-bullsh-sh-shit, I...I..I will be 100% again-again," in my broken stutter.

He responded, "Great! You are going to need that attitude," while wearing a smile that said, "you sir, are fucked."

That night, long after Mel had gone home for the night, but before the nightly vampire would arrive, I laid there in the darkness and almost broke down crying.

The weight of it was finally settling in. I thought about the fact that I could have easily not woken up that morning. I thought about everything I had been working towards, my book, now a few months old, being the last thing I may ever write, how good it felt to tell a joke on stage while hosting an event, just two months ago.

My dream of one day using my words to make a living, instead of my back, was all slipping away. I pulled myself together before I started crying, because at the time, I felt like if I started, I may never stop.

I didn't have time to feel sorry for myself. I reminded myself that bad luck happens, that I have been pretty lucky thus far, and that I couldn't let Mel and the kids see me like this.

To be clear, I am not one of those dads that teaches his kids, especially his son, that it's not OK to cry. I fully believe that men can cry, that men crying is healthy, etc....

That being said, I would never let my kids see me cry, I would never let my kids see me break down, I would never let my kids see me be weak.

I'm their father, I have one all-encompassing job: to make them feel safe, to make them feel like their dad can do anything, to make them feel like their dad is superhuman... The way a dad should be.

Deep inside their heads, they know that I'm not superhuman, but I'd be damned if I was going to show them proof first hand. Life can and will be hard, soon enough they are going to face real pain and defeat. They don't need to see real pain and defeat in their father.

So, I pulled my shit together and made the decision that I was going to be OK, I wasn't going to feel the pain of it, and neither was anyone else.

For the rest of my stay in the hospital, I was up-beat and congenial. Whatever they were doing to me, no matter how humiliating or painful, I stuttered my way through a joke.

I was three days into the hospital stay when I finally got to eat again, but not before jumping through some hoops.

The occupational therapist was a tall, blonde, transgendered woman with a sense of humor, but also took her job very seriously. I only mention that she was transgendered because she probably wasn't. I really have no way of knowing if she was or wasn't a genetic female, but she had just enough physical cues that I wasn't sure. I had been in the hospital for a few days now and I was completely bored shitless, so for the sake of my sanity and boredom, she was transgendered...

Anyway, she had me take the same tests all three of the doctors, I was now seeing twice daily, were giving me, plus one. She had me take a drink of water and watched me swallow it.

As you have read in the previous pages, I was eating when I started to realize (thanks to Google) that I had a stroke, and my first night there I had "Jack in the Box." If I could swallow that, I could swallow anything. All of this had been told to every doctor and nurse involved, but finally I was vindicated. The person whose job it was to see if I could eat or not had witnessed me swallow something and I hadn't aspirated it into my lungs.

This, of course, was a shallow victory. Soon after seeing the occupational therapist, I was delivered my first meal in two days, heart healthy lasagna and steamed green beans.

I don't know if you have had "heart healthy" lasagna or not, but in case you have not had the pleasure... Remember middle school lunch lasagna? Well, it was a little like that if you removed the processed cardboard taste leaving no taste at all.

Day four and nothing changed. They were no longer doing any tests, just filling me full of fluids, checking my blood pressure every three hours, and taking blood twice a day. No new info, not even a lecture from the doctors, just boredom and "That 70's Show" reruns while I drug the IV tree back and forth to the bathroom every twenty minutes or so.

That night, my friend Trisha came to visit. Trisha is an emergency room nurse at a competing hospital and a highly qualified health care professional.

She had me use the "call button" to get the floor nurse to visit and requested a print out of all my paperwork. The nurse on duty that night, let us call her "Debbie," was new. She never said she was new, but it was obvious from her demeanor and lack of confidence that she had not been at this hospital long, or possibly in the profession long, but had been well-trained.

When Debbie was face-to-face with Trisha, Trisha full of confidence and authoritative bearing, born of many years of practical experience, she folded like a house of cards following Trisha's orders, as if they had been carved into stone tablets and carried down the mountain by Moses himself.

Trisha had Debbie print out hard copies of every bit of paperwork since I first showed up in the emergency room, then excused Debbie and closed the door to give us some privacy.

For the first time since all of this happened, someone who knew what they were doing sat down and fully explained everything. Everything that had been happening inside my body when I was having the stroke, every test that I had taken, and what all those tests really meant, and she explained all of it in plain English.

She gave me some advice, "Get a primary care doctor and get out of here as soon as you can. It's impossible to rest and heal in a hospital."

Going home...

The next morning, I requested that the doctor in charge see me to discuss getting me the hell out of there.

This turned into an ordeal. There were three doctors in charge of my care: the staff neurologist, the staff cardiologist, and staff general physician.

The neurologist saw no reason not to release me as all my blood work had returned to normal. The cardiologist didn't give a fuck one way or another and seemed pissed that he had to see me again. The general physician didn't want to discharge me until he saw proof that I had procured a primary care doctor, gave me two more lectures about partying, three lectures about remembering to take my daily medications, and generally seemed to think that I was a complete moron incapable of wiping my own ass without his help.

About 4pm, a nurse came to my room to remove my IV, remove my heart monitor, and start the process of discharging me.

I had spent five days with these nurses, even with my diminished ability to talk, I was still me and had made friends will all of the nursing staff by telling jokes and never being difficult. So, I chatted up the nurse discharging me into telling what had happened with the doctors. The general physician had pleaded his case that he was in charge and I should stay until I found a primary care doctor, but the neurologist won the day. I had been there for a stroke and after all, this was his field and he felt it was doing me more harm than good keeping me in the hospital.

I got dressed in my clothes and walked out under my own power, I was really happy about it.

The first thing I noticed, while riding the elevator down to the lobby, was that five days in bed wreaks havoc on the body. I was winded from just walking down the hall and out to the parking lot.

In the parking lot, Mel reached out to me with the car keys with a look that said, "Are you driving?"

I took the keys and unlocked the driver's door...

We were half of a block into the drive when I told her, "I'm going to be OK, I've got this."

I will never forget the look of relief on her face. Mel knows me better than any person alive or dead, she knows I can drive anything, anywhere, anytime, it's central to my confidence. I am first and foremost, a driver.

Before going home, we had to go to the pharmacy and pick up the pills that would now be a constant clock that would measure my days. This one you take as soon as you wake up, this one you take at noon every day, this one you take before bed every night...

The pharmacy was my first interaction with the public and it didn't go particularly well.

I walked up to the counter and tried to give the girl working there my information and it all came out as a stuttering word jumble of incoherent nonsense. I almost cracked as Mel jumped in and explained the situation, gave the girl my info, and got my prescriptions.

The next two days were filled with watching TV while Mel found doctors for me to see.

In those first two days, I also experienced my first anxiety attack.

This was not being stressed out over a job interview, or a social situation, this was a physical attack.

I was sitting in my office doing my speech therapy, therapy consisting of reading a sentence then typing it out while also reading the sentence aloud, and my field of vision started to darken. At first, I thought one of the shop lights had burnt out, so I looked up at the overhead lights. That's when I noticed the room had not only gotten darker, but my perspective had skewed. My depth perception had gone completely haywire, objects that were far away were somehow moving toward me. Objects that were close to me were moving away and falling in and out of focus. As this was happening, I started to notice a tingling in the top of my head that moved its way down my face. As it moved, it changed from a tingle to a numbness as it hit my chest and arms, then turned into a vibrating tingle as it moved into my legs.

I almost fell over as a wave of dizziness and nausea fell over me and I realized I was sweating so badly I had soaked through my shirt and shorts.

"This is it," I thought, I was sure I was having a massive heart attack.

I sat there, elbows propped up on my desk holding my head up with both hands, for what was probably several minutes, but felt like hours, until the symptoms passed.

I really should have dialed 911, or at least called out for help, but I couldn't move or speak.

The event left me so completely shaken I couldn't even talk to Mel about it until the next day, nor could I sleep that night.

The next day we went to see my new primary care physician. When I saw this new doctor for the first time, I was expecting new blood tests, an MRI, a CT scan, something... But no, all my previous information was used, mainly the tests that had been done in the first 24 hours after having the stroke.

This really bothered me. How were they to know if I was healing? How were they to know if anything had changed?

I felt like complete shit, I couldn't walk across the room without being winded, and I had made the mistake of reading my test results from the tests done on my heart, those results filling every moment of conscious thought.

One of those tests had read, "Abnormal valve function."

And another note in my records read, "Abnormal heart rhythm."

None of these issues had been brought to me by the cardiologist while I was in the hospital, and no one had addressed it since.

I described the episode that had happened the previous night and the doctor explained that after a major medical event such as this, it's normal for the patient to suffer from anxiety. He prescribed a Xanax knock-off while telling me that if the anxiety attacks persisted, we would have to look to long term drug therapy, something I was adamantly against.

He attempted to address the abnormal heart valve issue and abnormal heart rate issue, but couldn't, as he admitted that cardiology was not his specialty. He asked if I would like a referral to a cardiologist who might be able to answer some of these questions?

Fuck yes, I would like a referral, it's my fucking heart!?!

Weeks passed, and I didn't die. I started to speak correctly again, though it took a lot of effort, and I learned to write again.

For a couple of weeks, I took the temporary medication for anxiety as the attacks happened, then started to ween myself off them in favor of dealing with the PTSD I had suffered, head on.

There were some truly dark moments, like locking myself in a Chipotle bathroom for 30 minutes while I used up an entire roll of toilet paper to clean the sweat off my body, then finally leaving the restaurant without ordering food because I could not get the room to stop tilting sideways. Then, sitting in my truck for another 20 minutes with the air-conditioning turned up to full blast as I listened to the "Joe Rogan Experience" podcast at top volume so that I could concentrate enough to drive home. But even then, I felt like I was winning the war on anxiety attacks while not gaining a habit, as the anxiety drugs are highly addictive.

Learning about people...

As all of this was going on, I was contacted by more friends, acquaintances, and total strangers than at any other time in my life. People were coming out of the woodwork to offer sympathy, advice, and help, and I'm thankful for all of them.

But, it was truly a study in first-world humanity in its many forms.

My close friends, the people who really know me, pretty much left me alone. We had all talked at least once while I was in the hospital, they knew that I wasn't comfortable talking, that I wasn't comfortable seeing anyone, and they respected that fact. If I needed them, they were a call or text away, and would have dropped everything to help, but that's not me. I didn't need help. I needed time. Time to heal. Time to figure out this new reality and deal with it my own way.

There were many other well-meaning well-wishers, people with truly wonderful hearts who wanted nothing more than to see me get better, but didn't/don't really know me, who tried very hard to force their help on me. There were some trying moments with these people. I understood their need to help. I understood their motives were genuine and pure. But, I had just suffered a stroke that had left me incapable of conveying both my appreciation of their concern and my need to be left alone to deal with this.

The third group were the self-important dick faces. I ran into very few of these, but one would have been too many. These were the guys (and yes, they were always guys) who completely ignored my social media posts (including video) about what was going on and how it sent me into an anxiety spiral to talk about it. It was always guys on underpowered metric café bikes, every one of them were those "trying too hard," "wannabees" who demanded that I tell them the entire story start to finish as I was trying to leave a bar. It's no wonder you super-creeps are always falling in love with lesbians, you are so narcissistic there is no way you can even pick up on the most basic social cues.

The next, and fortunately much smaller group of people, were people who were trying to use my affliction to garner sympathy for their own (mostly made-up) afflictions. These people would write messages that always started with- "I know what you are going through," pay a bit of lip service to my stroke, then tell me about their auto-immune disorder that no doctor can diagnose because the healthcare industry wants them to die because only they know the truth... I got good at shutting these people down quickly with a "can't type... stroke."

The last, and smallest group of people were people I really thought were my friends, though friends I had not seen in a very long time. These "friends" waited a few weeks, until it seemed like I was on the mend, then asked (via text) how I was doing? Due to a misplaced sense of obligation, dictated by long standing friendship, I answered honestly. I told them everything. The anxiety, the fear, and disappointment at the many doctors not being able to tell me why this happened, my questionable heart, all of it.

Well, as I learned the hard way, some people you thought you were close to, just really want to hear, "I'm fine," as all four of these close friends who were so worried about how I was doing, failed to respond to my explanation of how I was doing, then quietly avoided me around town and on social media. If any of them are reading this, I'm sorry. "I'm fine..."

Getting answers...

Going to the cardiologist was my doctor's plan to alleviate some of my anxiety.

The first 10 minutes meeting with this new doctor helped. Then, it really didn't. The doctor was looking through my test results and telling me everything "looked great." Then, his demeanor changed and he spoke under his breath, "Well… I guess I might have overlooked that…"

I could tell by the look on his face that he had found something very wrong, and I called him on it, "What's going on Doc?"

He tried to look as relaxed as he could as he said, "Well…"

Then, stopped talking.

"Well, what? S-S-Spit it out Doc!"

As some of you know, I am not a very large person, but when I want to be, I am very intimidating. A lifetime of hard work and a hard life have made me as hard as a hammer, and just as dangerous.

I could tell the cardiologist didn't want to say anything. He was hooked into the same hospital system that the doctors who had treated me in the emergency room were. There was something I had not been told, and he knew it. But professional courtesy was weighing on him.

Well, those doctors who treated me were not here, and I sure as fuck was. I would be willing to bet that not one of those doctors has ever hit a man in anger, and I sure as fuck have.

The cardiologist seemed to understand instantly what his choices were, and that he didn't really have any.

"One of your tests showed an abnormality in your heart valve function, it's probably nothing, I probably would have missed it if I would have been treating you, but it's there, and we really should check it out."

I was still in a state of dead calm, a state I only get in just before I have a violent outburst, "OK, what the fuck does that mean?"

The doctor replied, "Well, it means we should order a nuclear stress test. If that test shows a problem, we may have to implant a monitor in your chest until we figure out what's wrong."

None of this helped with my new-found anxiety problem. Very much the opposite.

Outside of the emergency room, nothing moves quickly in the world of medicine. It moves even more slowly when they think you are going to stiff them on the bill.

Weeks went by while I waited to take tests, all the while I had to work a very physically demanding job right in the heart of the hardest and hottest part of the year, monsoon season in Arizona.

115 degrees Fahrenheit and high humidity.

Every day I was sure I was going to die.

I would wake up in the morning, smoke a cigar, drink coffee, get dressed, climb into my truck, and drive to "Quick Trip," for gas and coffee. I would have a panic attack somewhere between gas and coffee and find myself sitting in my truck with the air-conditioning running, with my head in my hands trying to control the fear, trying to slow my heart rate down.

This would also happen about every third pool I serviced. My heart would start racing, I would start sweating, and I would have to sit in the truck and try to calm down.

As you can imagine, thinking you are having seven to nine heart attacks a day is very time consuming, and does not in any way contribute to a happy and productive work environment.

While waiting for the tests on my heart, I got to meet with a neurologist and a hand surgeon. The neurologist was a "follow-up" to discuss the stroke, and the hand surgeon was because my doctor was completely stumped with regards to my finger problem. He had never seen these symptoms and it was time to look for help as the symptoms had not gotten any better.

First was the neurologist. I don't have insurance, as I have said previously, so shopping for a doctor who would take cash was a bit hit-and-miss.

We finally found a neurologist who was not only in our hospital's network (so he could easily access all of the tests that had been done) but would also accept cash.

As soon as Mel made the appointment, I understood why he was so flexible when it came to payment. His first name was Muhamad in one of the reddest of red states.

Well, to all my red friends, Dr. Muhamad was lovely. Not only did he explain my test results from the emergency room, he ordered new MRI's of my brain because my recovery was thus far "remarkable" in his words.

He spent most of the afternoon with me, showed me the videos of the original tests, and compared them with the new images. He showed me how my brain had rerouted blood flow from the blocked blood vessels to my damaged brain tissues. Something that is not supposed to happen, but there it was, in beautifully rendered high-definition.

Where the emergency room neurologist had told me I would never recover, Dr. Muhamad showed me the video evidence that there was no reason for me not to make a full recovery.

For the first time in all this pain and fear, I felt the first tinge of hope.

That night, for the first time since having a stroke, I didn't dream about having a stroke.

The anxiety attacks persisted.

Like clockwork, I would start to have one as soon as I put my truck into park at the gas station as I drove to work in the morning, and a second one as I started to eat my lunch around noon every day.

Sometimes they were mild, just a feeling of "wrongness," like I was not me and that I was looking through someone else's eyes. But most of the time, it looked and felt as if the very laws of physics had broken down, as if solid walls were moving of their own accord, that gravity was failing. Whatever room I was in was either about to blow itself apart, or even worse, that it was going to collapse in on me as if I had become some sort of human singularity where my gravity was pulling anything and everything toward me at unimaginable speed.

I would leave my sunglasses on as I entered the gas station so that no one would see the absolute terror in my eyes, as I stood there clutching the counter that housed the coffee makers, as if my very life depended on it, as the room and everyone in it tilted and heaved "funhouse mirror style" around me.

Most of the time I would not even remember paying for my morning coffee. I would find myself in my truck with the windows up and the air-conditioning on, a sweaty mess clutching the wheel for dear life and trying to think about where I was going next, as opposed to what I had just experienced, and all the while, telling myself that I was going to be "fine."

My next doctor's visit was to the hand surgeon. This was going to be an expensive one, this guy was at the top of his field after recently leaving the top hand surgery hospital in the country to start his own private practice here in Phoenix.

All of my doctor visits had been extremely expedient. I had not waited more than 15 minutes in a waiting room to date (yes, those Obama-care wait times are complete bullshit and political propaganda), until I waited to see this doctor. He was a "rock star" in his field, and you were going to pay the "rock star" premium waiting to see him.

I would have been pissed off at waiting over an hour, or I should say I was pissed off at waiting over an hour, until I saw the doctor.

He took one look at my hands, hands that had been seen by seven doctors who had no idea what was going wrong, and he said, "So, how long did you work in the oil field?"

Everything that was said after that was off the record. You see, George Bush signed an executive order that made it a crime for doctors to ask what chemicals oilfield workers are exposed to, Obama never got rid of the law, and Trump is too stupid to be able to read. So basically, the doctor can't say what caused it, but he has seen it, and I'm going to have it for the rest of my life.

There was good news though, it had a name, and it was treatable.

Finally, a doctor had connected all the dots. It was not just the "worst luck ever" that I suffered a kidney stone, diverticulitis, a stroke, and a small heart attack in less than three weeks.

Time to pay up!!

Doctor bills were starting to pile up.

The money I had made on the first book was now gone, and pool service, though it pays my regular monthly bills, was not going to cover pricey hand surgeons and cardiologists.

As a "stopgap," I had to fire up the art studio portion of my shop.

As many of you already know, but for those who don't, I dabble in glass and metal art. Mainly stained glass and metal sculpture, and neither are anything I have aspired to do professionally.

Working with steel or glass is meditation for me, they are activities I do when everything is already right with the world, and I am trying to continue that good feeling.

Doing it for money sucks. It takes away from the reason I do it.

But, desperate times call for desperate measures, and these bills were getting pretty fucking desperate.

In the weeks after the stroke, I had been learning about Viking style sword, knife, and axe making. Learning about these particular blacksmithing techniques was a small way for me to start to reclaim my manhood after finding out that I was far more weak and fragile than I had ever imagined.

Now, I'm a progressive person.

I'm all for feminism, I empathize with the plight of the transgendered, I think gay people should be able to marry, all that shit.

But, I am a masculine man. I love a good fight, internal combustion, firearms... In almost every way, I am a stereotype of the masculine man.

It wasn't a choice I made, I was born loving horsepower and pussy.

So, having a stroke, finding a very real weakness in my physiology, was fucking with me. I no longer felt like the man I knew. I no longer felt like I was the alfa who could protect his family.

As I said, to combat these feelings of inadequacy, these questions about my manhood, I turned to watching videos of blacksmithing and MMA, I reread "The "Iliad," and studied up on all of the great conquerors throughout history.

After a week or so of watching blacksmithing videos, I decided to forge my own knife.

My first one was way too big, way too cumbersome to use every day at work, so I based my second knife off of a tried and true 4" fixed blade design. That second knife worked great as a "do everything" work knife.

When I forged it, I had beat a "Valkyrie wing" into the steel and had crafted the handle from a skateboard I had ridden a year or so ago. The Valkyrie wing and the handle made from a skateboard were symbolic and important to me. The skateboard handle reminded me I still had things I wanted to grind, and the wing reminded me that I had just come close to dying in bed, and for me, there is just no worse way to die.

The blade was well received on social media, so much so, I have three knives to build as I write this.

A couple of days before I was scheduled to take a very important test on my heart, something called a "nuclear stress test," my good friend Claude sent a text wanting to take a day trip up north.

Claude is the person I ride motorcycles with the most. Every story you have read in my book, or on my blog site involved Claude.

I was trying to stay positive, I was trying to will this upcoming test to have positive results.

I kept telling myself, "I'm fine," "I'm going to be the man I was," "I am not weak," all the while my subconscious was screaming, "You are dying!"

Claude was one of the friends who left me alone while I was healing. But, he also knew enough time had passed, he had seen a couple of social media posts showing me taking short trips around town on my bike, and it was time for me to climb back on that horse and ride toward glory.

400 miles round trip.

For those who have never ridden a motorcycle, 400 miles is a long way. 400 miles is a marathon, testing both the rider's physical prowess, and his ability to keep his head in the game mile after mile. And on my bike, a suicide clutch having, hand shifting, brake failing, death machine, it was doubly so.

We hit all the usual spots. We stopped for beer at all the usual places, I even played with a wild tarantula at one spot.

For the first time since the stroke, we were two cowboys doing cowboy shit in the desert. I felt more like me than I had in months.

I wish that I could say that the ride was total freedom and escape, that for the first time I didn't think about the last two months, but it wasn't.

Halfway through the 400 miles, I broke down while drinking a beer next to a high-desert lake, and told Claude what it was really like, how I really felt.

The fear, the pain, the pills.

To Claude's credit, he pointed at the lake in front of us, pointed at the elk drinking near the water's edge, and said, "You are drinking a tall-boy on the side of a 7,000-foot mountain, you got to this mountain riding a crazy chopper, and you had a stroke less than two months ago. You couldn't even kill you."

It was some crazy cowboy shit to say, but I really needed to hear some crazy cowboy shit.

Several hours later, we were back in the Phoenix valley. Claude kept driving south down the "B-line" toward the east valley and I turned west on Shea Boulevard toward central Phoenix.

At the next light, I turned off into a Circle-K gas station to buy cigars and a water.

As I paid, all hell broke loose. As I have said, it was monsoon season and one of our famous monsoon storms had formed and was now battering the Circle-K with high winds and horizontal rain.

I stood there for about 15 minutes smoking a cigar and watching the rain from the safety of the store's cantilevered roof, before deciding to take my chances with the weather. I could have looked up the radar forecast on my phone, but Claude's words were still ringing in my ears.

No helmet, no face mask, no windshield, not even a front fender. It was just going to be the wind, the rain, blindness, cold wet fear, and me.

The storm chased me all 24 miles home and I rode through the worst of it. At one point, I jumped my bike over a tree that had been blown over and covered the road. After the third traffic light, I stopped stopping for the lights, for fear of being blown over, as I could only put one foot down to steady the bike with my suicide clutch setup.

I was soaked, I was cold to the bone, I was blind, and I wasn't stopping. I was going to live, if it killed me.

Time to face the music...

I showed up to the cardiologist's office smelling like stale beer, and hungover from a day of riding motorcycles in the mountains and drinking heavily. Mel was a little pissed at me and even commented that I should have taken it a little easier the day before I was given the tests.

She was back to work, summer break was over, and it was time for her to resume educating Arizona's youth.

This was my first doctor's visit and medical testing that she wasn't going to be there for, and I sure as shit was not going to do it completely straight.

I couldn't be drunk. Shit, I couldn't even have a cup of coffee before the test or it would foul the results and I would have to take it again. But, no one said shit about being completely hungover and physically beat from a long ride, so that's exactly how I showed up.

I call this type of hangover a "category 3." It's not really painful. I don't feel sick. I just feel like I'm mildly depressed, like anything could happen to me without caring. I just want to sleep and be left alone.

It was the perfect state of being for three to five hours in a hospital.

The test was straightforward. They shot me up with radioactive dye, then waited 45 minutes (me watching shitty game shows next to sad old women in their early 60's) as they waited for the dye to flow around my body.

After the 45 minutes, they took me into a room where I had to lie completely still as they shot pictures of my heart as it pumped blood in a rested state.

This took about 15 minutes.

Then, for the next 2.5 hours, I watched TV as they took one elderly woman after another back to take the same test.

Finally, they called my name and took me into a room with a treadmill. They hooked many, many sensors up to my chest and back and then had me start walking on the treadmill.

I walked at a brisk pace for the next 20 minutes. The goal of the treadmill was to get your heart rate up to 150 beats per minute.

They had access to my medical records and assured me I wouldn't need to run; a brisk walk should do the trick.

Well, they were wrong.

They cranked up the treadmill to its top speed, all the while keeping a close eye on the EKG.

I ran flat out for 15 minutes.

I could not tell you how long it's been since I ran flat out for 15 straight minutes. Thirty-three years of skateboarding has ruined my knees and my willingness to feel the pain of running.

My heart finally hit the magic number, 150 beats per minute.

As they slowed the treadmill down, injected me with more radioactive dye, and started to disconnect the leads for the sensors from my chest, the nurse in charge commented about how I was in great shape.

I was winded, my voice was still affected by the stroke, but I tried to make a joke, "Y-y-you h-have obviously not read my f-f-f-file."

Shortly after the treadmill, they rushed me back into the camera room to have me lie down and lie still the same way I had four hours earlier.

Fifteen minutes later, they were telling me to get dressed and letting me know that a doctor would be calling me with the results in five to nine days.

Five to nine days is a very long time when you are thinking about your heart, and more importantly, if it's going to just stop working at any minute.

I poured myself into my work more intensely than I ever have during this time, even though the doctors and common sense both recommended that I relax and try not to work hard.

I had to, if I stopped working, I started thinking, and thinking was turning into the enemy.

I stopped sleeping.

I stopped eating.

I was work and worry.

Nothing else.

During the week or so of waiting, a friend of mine got it in his head that he really wanted to see the upcoming total eclipse that was happening in North America in August.

It was Tuesday night, the night we spend our time drinking cheap beer and talking about motorcycles, and my friend, "The Professor," would not shut up about this eclipse, "Something, something totality, "something, something Wyoming."

Honestly, I wasn't really paying attention as my mind was completely preoccupied with waiting for the results of the tests on my heart.

He laid it out in details: a nine-day trip to see the eclipse, Devils Tower, the Black Hills...

I think, as I said, I wasn't really paying attention.

He was halfway through his sales pitch when I looked from my beer and said, "I'm in."

He said something along the lines of, "Really?"

And I said, "Yes, as long as these tests go well, and my doctor says I'm physically capable of going, I'm going."

I had not talked to Mel yet, I really couldn't afford to do this, given the time in the hospital where I wasn't making money and the ever-accumulating medical bills, but I was going.

Three days later I got a call from the cardiologist.

"Mr. Keeley?"

"Yes."

"This is Dr #@$%^ from Arrowhead Cardiology."

"Yes."

"Mr. Keeley, I'm just calling to inform you that your tests went well, there is no sign of a future heart attack, and the damage from your last incident has healed perfectly."

"So, I'm going to be OK?"

"Yes sir, you are going to be fine."

Well shit, guess I'm going to Wyoming...

The good news about my heart had not stopped the anxiety attacks, as my primary doctor had hoped it would. He began to look and speak to me as if I was purposely causing these traumatic events, just to spite him.

I didn't want drugs, though, I'm sure this was a new concept to him, I wanted control.

He wanted me on a long-term medication as a solution.

I wanted "me," as a solution.

As much as I respected him as a doctor, I was going to win this battle.

Hey, I love drugs.

Drugs have been a huge part of my life.

But, there is a time for drugs, and this was not the time.

I was not expanding my mind. I was not adding icing to a good time cake. There was a serious problem with my brain and how I was processing information, and drugs were not going to fix it. Not this time.

My doctor was completely against my idea that nine days of motorcycle camping in the northwest was one of the keys to my recovery.

He was completely in favor of me taking nine days off work, pointing out the fact that I had only taken one week off to recover from a stroke, and that was just not enough time. But, he really thought that riding a motorcycle in places like Colorado, Wyoming, and South Dakota, given my anxiety issues, was a really bad idea.

I told none of his misgivings to Mel, I didn't have to. She knew what needed to be done. She knew that I was struggling to reclaim the man I was, and the man I was, would take an underfunded, motorcycle, camping trip at the worst possible time with almost no supplies.

For the next month, I worked almost constantly to make enough money to make the trip happen. I was still struggling with medical bills and I really needed to sink some money into my bike, if it was going to survive 3,000 miles of sustained mountain riding, fully loaded. I needed to be able to eat at least twice a day. I needed to be able to buy fuel on the trip, and I really couldn't afford to do any of it.

But, things always work out if you work hard enough and you really need them to.

I was able to do a full service on the bike the day before we left, I was able to order enough dehydrated food for two meals a day on the trail off Amazon, and my favorite pool customer gave me a $500 prepaid AMEX card to cover gas and incidentals. On top of that, I had managed to save $200 cash, making and selling knives.

$77.77 per day to cover gas, restaurants, visitor fees, whatever... I could do that.

OK, I couldn't really do that. I wanted to. I needed to, but it really wasn't possible. Fortunately, the other guys on the ride, and my friends who couldn't make it, knew that, even if I had convinced myself otherwise. They also knew that if nothing else, I was proud, and secretly passed the hat to cover all of my lodging and camping fees.

Highway 666 and fresh meat...

For the last two years, my friends and I have gone to a Moto Guzzi rally in the (very) small town of Datil, New Mexico.

For those who don't endlessly obsess about motorcycles, Moto Guzzis are the oldest motorcycle manufacturer in Italy, and Datil, New Mexico isn't really a town.

Moto Guzzis are a greasy mix of motorcycle and obsolete car technology with model names, that call forth images of a chlamydia diagnoses and men you would chase away from your sister.

Datil, New Mexico is a gas station/meat market/general store/restaurant/rustic campground with a population of under 30 people, that occupies an intersection of two New Mexico highways. Two highways that both lead absolutely nowhere.

You can't call Datil the middle of nowhere, because the middle of nowhere, is still more populated and better known than Datil, New Mexico.

This year, the Moto Guzzi rally in Datil was going to happen on the same weekend as the start of our nine-day trip to see the full solar eclipse, so of course, we made the trip to Datil our starting point.

Plus, given the fact that the Datil rally was well-known long in advance, and many of our friends who couldn't make the entire nine-day trip had already planned for Datil, and planned to ride with us at least that far, gave us a much more appropriate and fun-filled send-off.

Datil was Datil: an incredible steak dinner, drunkenly stealing wood for the campfire, and the usual campfire stories about motorcycle exploits long past.

Last year we raged with alcohol-fueled dancing around the campfire, animated stories while passing around 80-proof liquor, and laughter that could be heard two counties away, if any county near Datil contained any population to hear it.

This year it was more subdued, as everyone was anxious about the next eight days of motorcycle camping to come, and all of the challenges known and unknown.

Saturday, the first full day of the Datil rally, we got word that Scott wasn't going to make it.

Scott had problems at work and just couldn't take the day off. How much fun is Scott? He is so much fun that we were going to spend another day in Datil to wait for him, even though if he showed up, he would only be there one night and was not going on the big trip with us.

I personally was in favor of staying another night either way, I didn't see a point in leaving midafternoon on Saturday, after a full morning of visiting the VLA (Very Large Array, a very large series of radio telescopes near Datil), the morning and early afternoon Moto Guzzi festivities surrounding the rally, and the many beers I had drank while waiting for Scott.

But, I wasn't running this rodeo.

Matter of fact, I may not have even voiced my opinion on the matter.

I didn't want to be in charge.

Honestly, I really didn't even want to have a voice in how this shit was going to go.

Every minute of my life for the last two months had been a fight to quantify my reality, I was tired, I was beaten down by the effort of trying to be whole.

All I wanted to do was ride my motorcycle and let shit fall where it may.

While struggling to drunkenly repack my bike, the boys had been busy making friends. They had met and befriended, PJ and her dad Phil. PJ was a female rider in her mid-40's from northern Colorado, and her dad, Phil, was a rider in his early 70's from North Dakota.

Every year PJ and Phil would meet up in Colorado and ride to Datil, while drinking cheap beer and spending the most quality time a father and daughter could ever hope to.

Most of the people who frequent the Datil rally don't like me. It's not their fault, I don't blame them, they are just not my people.

The average Datil attendee has never seen heaven in the bottom of a cheap aluminum can filled with even cheaper beer, they have never had night of razorblades, mirrors, and powdery drugs.

But PJ and Phil swilled cheap beer like it was mother's milk, told dirty jokes, and appreciated busting balls.

Frankly, they were so cool I was shocked my friends found them.

PJ owns a house directly on our route to seeing the eclipse, and in true beer fueled biker fashion, she offered up her home and a home-cooked meal to help us on our way.

Yes, we are this slow...

We left Datil in midafternoon, I don't know what time it was, as I said, I was pretty drunk. But, we left in midafternoon on Saturday with the plan of making it as far as we could and getting a hotel.

The problem with "our" plan was as follows. The night before, we road Arizona highway 666, the longest continuous series of switch-backs on any road in the United States of America, aka, the Devil's Highway, 1,100 curves in 95 miles, every one of them will kill you. It's a marathon of butt clenching, peg dragging, adrenalin pumping madness, if you were on a sport-bike. On fully loaded bikes ready to camp for nine days, it was more than a workout.

The second problem was that we ate, drank, and were merry after riding Highway 666.

The third was that we started way too late.

Late in the day, after playing tourist and rally attendee, is no way to start hundreds of miles of riding across high plains and nothingness. It's just daunting to look back at the fun you were having in the face of eternal flat, if it isn't first thing in the morning.

But we trudged on.

Mile after boring mile through New Mexico.

We finally found a reason to wake up from the lethargy of endless plains and a late start by way of a real city, Albuquerque, NM.

The only problem with finding ourselves in the city was that "The Professor," the man who had planned this trip, had made the entire trip possible by strength of his will alone, had not quite found his groove when it came to lead four, tired, road weary bikers, through rush hour traffic, yet.

This was not a failing on his part, leading a group of bikes is hard.

It's stressful in ways that most people will never understand. Everyone who rides, wants to ride their way. They want to pick their path through traffic, they want to set the speed with which they do it, they want to travel at the speed that feels right to them and their bike.

Leading, you have to guess all of that. You can't feel everything every rider is feeling, you can't guess how every rider's bike is vibrating or sounding. All you can do is feel how your bike is doing and hope everyone else is also in that sweet spot between speed and vibration (they are not, they really are not).

Then you add in the fact that it was nighttime, and not being able to see anything in those tiny little vibrating motorcycle mirrors in traffic...

I'm not going to second guess The Professor, we all made it safe and sound. But, maybe, if there is a next time, maybe let's not try and pass every car on the road.

I love going 85-95 mph, I really do. But, it's a lot more fun alone on a road, I know.

If I had been leading, we would have been going ten under the speed limit, and I assure you, it would have been equally, if not more, irritating.

We made it safely out of Albuquerque going way too fast. By now, we had been on the road for six or seven hours, it was pitch black, and all of us were dreaming of the town of Las Vegas, New Mexico on the border of New Mexico and Colorado.

Why were we dreaming of a town none of us (and you) had ever heard of? Because, deep in the heart of Albuquerque, we had stopped for gas and as a group, we decided that that's as far as we should go, given how late it had become.

When I said "we," that was a bit of a misnomer. As I said, I had removed myself from the democratic process, and while the voting was in session, I was standing next to the gas station bathroom drinking two "airplane bottles" of vodka and smoking a cigar.

Here is an unsolicited "pro-tip" for all of the people who may travel around the USA and are wondering whether or not the gas station they have stopped at is in a good neighborhood or not: If the gas station sells one-ounce bottles (airplane bottles) of hard liquor and loose cigarettes, lock your shit up and watch your back, you are in "the hood."

This wasn't a problem for me, though I now live in a very nice part of town, I was born in the hood, and I really feel more comfortable in the hood.

The hood doesn't try to rob a guy on a motorcycle who is trying to hide his public drinking. The hood understands this behavior and respects it.

We had about 50 miles left to get to Las Vegas, New Mexico when The Professor's balls out, pass anything on the road style, caught up to him, and by way of association, us.

Highway 25 between Albuquerque and Las Vegas, New Mexico was all up hill. Halfway between the two cities was the start of the Rocky Mountains.

The Professor chose to address this elevation change by going 95 mph, and in doing so, his trusty 30-year-old 750 Honda (fully loaded for nine days of camping), started blowing thick, white smoke.

I know that a majority of people reading this know nothing about what smoke looks like what, when it comes to a car or motorcycle, but since you are already reading this, allow me to educate you.

If your vehicle is producing black smoke, you are burning lots of gas. Your carburetor, injectors, or computer is fucked up.

If your vehicle is producing gray smoke, it's water or antifreeze. Your radiator, water pump, or head gasket is fucked up.

If it's white smoke (the worst kind of smoke), generally your entire engine is fucked up.

But, in smaller motors, it can be the breather. All engines have a breather. Your car does, but they call it a PCV valve. You have probably heard of this part if you have ever had your oil changed at a shifty, disreputable oil change place (your PCV should last the life of the vehicle and does not need to be changed at every oil change).

Basically, as all the moving parts of your engine move and rotate, they build up tremendous air pressure as they move, and the engine needs to get rid of all that air. That's what your PCV valve does, and what the engine breather does on a motorcycle.

If you overwork your car, the PCV valve will belch oil out of the engine, but, with the miracle of plumbing, that oil is returned back to the engine and you are none the wiser.

Because motorcycle engines are smaller and room for plumbing is at a minimum, if you run the engine hard enough for the breather to belch oil, it usually ends up spilling out from the engine someplace you would rather not have it.

In the case of a 1980 Honda CB750, that place would be the exhaust header. The single hottest spot on the motorcycle.

The real problem in seeing white, oily smoke pouring out of the lead bike on a motorcycle trip, is that no one thinks, "Oh, he is overloaded and running too fast, he must have loaded up the breather."

It also happened to be 10pm in the mountains, and no one could see shit.

It took at least 45 minutes for four guys, who intimately know small displacement engines, to figure out that the 30-year-old Honda had not suffered a trip-ending, catastrophic engine failure.

That's right, 45 minutes in the freezing cold, using our phones as flashlights, me getting progressively soberer, we finally figured out that he was going too hard with too much weight for an old motorcycle.

To be honest, as I laid down on the cold asphalt, getting progressively soberer, looking for the real problem, I almost wanted his bike to have shit itself. If it had, the trip would be over. If it had, I would no longer have to pretend I was strong enough to do this ride.

But it didn't.

I was going to face the cold mountain night for at least 50 more miles.

We made it to Las Vegas without any more white smoke, but not any more weirdness.

As I mentioned, "we" had voted on staying at a hotel that night, the only hotel stay of the trip. The reason "we" (as I said, I had not taken part in the decision-making process) was because PJ had recommended this particular hotel.

Why had PJ recommended this particular hotel in a town, a nowhere town on the edge of the desert and the mountains, this town that seemed to be made up of primarily hotels, because of her last visit, it was cheap and biker friendly.

Well, as time moves on, shit happens.

I'm not going to name the hotel we stayed at, I don't want to badmouth them, though I'm almost sure that it no longer matters, as it has to be out of business at the time of this writing.

We had called ahead from Albuquerque (when I say we, I mean one of us who had not completely checked out, probably The Professor), and reserved two rooms, two beds per room, for four men.

When we showed up, we were greeted by a morbidly obese man in his mid-30's, with no shirt on, holding a small dog, and our reservation had turned into one room with two twin beds.

At first, our group tried to argue with the man, tried to explain that we had called ahead, but it was all for not. Yes, he has the extra room, but had not bothered to clean it, and somehow this was our fault. He was visibly angry with us because he had not cleaned the second room.

We calmed him down explaining that it was obviously our fault, and how we would be more than happy to take the second, uncleaned, room.

This seemed to satisfy him for a bit, that was until we asked if we could get clean towels.

We didn't get clean towels.

In our last desperate act, as we left the office, Dino asked (half joking), if there was anywhere that delivered food to the hotel.

The fat, shirtless, small dog carrying man's reply was priceless, and descriptive of our experience thus far with hotel, "There isn't any restaurants in this town." Dino started to protest, pointing out that Google said this was a town of 29,000 people... I stopped him as I realized how fruitless his effort was going to be, and we walked to our rooms: one clean, one very much the opposite.

Dino found food. There were several pizza joints that would deliver to this hotel, he even offered to pay as a means of easing everyone's pain at what we had just dealt with.

Dino and The German's room was the clean room. It was close to the office, and though we had asked for adjoining rooms, as we found out, even towels were too much to ask for.

The Professor's and my room was all the way across the parking lot. Oh, how I wish that was the only indignity.

The Professor's room was not only a smoking room (not a problem for me), it obviously had a mold problem, as it smelled like a damp basement.

When the manager had said he forgot to clean the room, he was not joking. The first thing we noticed was the mold smell, the second was the pile of petrified McDonald's French-fries standing tall in the deep shag, like a potato rendered Stonehenge.

I unpacked my shit, the little I would need to unpack for a one-night stay in a hotel, mainly a bottle of Tito's vodka, a bottle of cranberry juice, and my emergency toilet paper, as the roll in the room's bathroom was nearly exhausted, and I really didn't feel like dealing with whatever insanity was running the front office.

I mixed myself a cocktail in one of the complimentary plastic cups (fortunately the last occupant, the French-fry monument builder, had left two, sterilized, prepackaged cups, unmolested). Then, I walked across the parking lot to Dino and The German's room to eat the pizza Dino had ordered from one of the numerous pizza places the hotel manager had assured us didn't exist.

Jokes were told, pizza was eaten, my cocktail was finished.

The boys had talked a good game about getting drunk that night, earlier in the ride. But, road exhaustion was taking them, and I could see it.

They were heading to bed.

Dino even apologized for not being able to stay up and drink.

It would have been nice to have company, but I understood. The guys were on a motorcycle trip, I was on a different trip altogether, and I couldn't blame them for being tired.

I walked back to The Professor's and my room. The professor was stretched out on the bed closest to the door. I don't know if he was pretending to sleep or actually sleeping, it really didn't matter.

I made a fresh cocktail and sat outside the room in one of those plastic lawn chairs, drinking and smoking a cigar while watching traffic go by, as I drank my way through a half fifth of Tito's.

At one point, I texted my friends, Bob and Jenna.

I texted them a small portion of what I had been writing so far on this trip. But really, I was just drunk, lonely, and scared.

I chose my drunk text's well, the two people I wouldn't have to apologize to. They knew I was drunk, they knew I was lonely. They would understand.

Deep into the night, long after I should have been in bed, I befriended a stray cat. Befriending a stray cat does not mean petting a stray cat. It means that a stray cat has chosen to spend time near you, chosen to acknowledge that you exist, and that you exist on the same plane of reality as him.

I was at the point where I had to debate myself on whether or not to make another cocktail, I didn't. Instead, I followed my new cat friend out of the parking lot and into an alley.

I don't know how far I followed the cat, the entire time telling it all of my fears, but it was long enough that I didn't recognize my surroundings and wasn't sure if I knew my way back to the hotel.

The cat finally stopped and let me scratch its ears. I thanked it for being a good friend as I started to cry and started to make my way back through the alleys to the hotel. I found The Professor sleeping, true sleep this time, I undressed and fell fast asleep.

Moto hospitality at its finest...

The next morning was hard. I was hungover, I hadn't slept much, as much as I should have, and The Professor had to wake me up.

When he woke me up, he led me to believe that everyone was waiting on me. If you know me, there is nothing I hate more than anyone having to wait on me.

I pride myself on being on time, and not being the cause of anyone having to wait. Forcing others to have to wait, because you were not ready, is super disrespectful. It's like saying, "I don't give a fuck about your time."

I drunkenly jumped into the shower. I did it with so much haste I didn't even remember or notice that there were no clean towels.

I toweled off with my clothes from the last day, then quickly repacked my bag, and then strapped everything back to the bike without one thought of my surroundings. It was absolute tunnel vision.

As soon as the bike was packed, I calmed down a little bit and started to realize that I was not what everyone was waiting on, not even close.

The Professor had underestimated my ability to function with a severe hangover and my willingness to pack my shit rapidly under pressure.

The German handed me a gas station travel cup of coffee as I watched everyone just start to pack their bikes.

I sat down in one of those plastic chairs and lit a cigar and sipped the coffee while thinking, "What the fuck, man?"

I didn't have much time to be pissed at The Professor for waking me up and making me feel like I had to rush, because before I was halfway through my cup of coffee, everyone started pointing and shouting to the south.

At first, we thought the gas station, where The German had bought our coffee, was on fire. After further inspection, we realized that it was a mid-80's Ford pick-up, sitting at the gas pumps, that was on fire.

We watched an entire melodrama unfold as the boys packed their bikes: people were running, firemen were showing up, and the fire almost putting itself out as the firemen pulled out their hoses.

It was the perfect, super hungover, being in a strange place, in a strange mindset, morning entertainment.

Finally, an hour later, everyone was ready to go.

Food, and the procurement of food, is a constant hassle on any trip. With these guys, it was less so. No one had a goofy diet they were on, no one was a vegan, no was "claiming" a gluten intolerance, but even with guys who can eat anything, it's still a pain in the ass.

The German took the lead in the breakfast endeavor by googling from his phone, "Doesn't an everything bagel with cream cheese and coffee sound good right now?" he said in his thick German accent... Well no, it really didn't sound that good, but I was in no shape to argue, nor did I have any compulsion to.

We all saw the sign that said "breakfast" leaving the hotel, and we all ignored it. The German had taken the lead and we were going to follow. He took the initiative, when the rest of us didn't, and we were going to respect that.

Twenty-five minutes later, and eight round-a-bouts, we realized we had taken a very thorough tour of the college at the center of Las Vegas, NM without finding any "Einstein Bagels." Google had fucked The German, and us with him.

Full circle, back to the hotel we went, when we once again saw the sign that said "breakfast" literally right next door to the hotel.

Well, the place didn't have the "everything bagels," but what they had was some of the best Mexican/New Mexican/Native American food I had ever tasted, at unreal prices.

I ordered the three-breakfast taco deal for $6.99 for no other reason than it was cheap and looked filling. What I got was three tacos filled with diced ham, grilled hatch chilies, eggs, and cheese wrapped in Navajo frybread. This wasn't a meal, this was a feast, and all for under eight-bucks.

If you are in the southwest and planning to eat, please follow my advice: no matter what the place looks like, if everyone at the restaurant is Mexican or Native American, grab a seat and a menu. You can thank me later.

Once again, we were not on the road until after noon, due to morning rituals and slow loading of motorcycles.

Colorado is legendarily beautiful, but on the freeway, it just looks like everywhere else, and we had a full day of freeway.

Just around dark, we made it to PJ's neighborhood. PJ lived in a stretch of Colorado near the northern border of Colorado and Wyoming, dominated by industrial farming. It was one of those places all across the Midwest that could be anywhere, as long as anywhere was Central Michigan, Wisconsin, Nebraska, Iowa, South Dakota, North Dakota, etc....

But, some places are not about the scenery, they are about the people, and PJ and her dad Phil had already shown themselves to not only be good people, but fun and funny people.

We got gas about two miles from PJ's house and sent her a text. We asked what we could bring, and her only reply was, "Hamburger buns."

We hit the grocery store right across the road from the gas station and Dino and I went in and bought buns. We also tried to buy beer. We are grown men, we are going to show up with beer.

Well, trying to buy beer in the grocery store in northern Colorado was one of those experiences that reminds you that the USA is a collection of states, and the rules change state to state.

In AZ, you can buy beer anywhere. Every gas station, every grocery store, every drug store, literally everywhere.

Colorado? Not so much. We were politely informed that you could not buy beer at the grocery store, we needed to go to the beer store, a short walk across the parking lot.

No problem. We didn't mind a short walk, we had been sitting on motorcycles all day, after all, a short walk would be good for us. What they forgot to mention was that buying beer in CO on Sunday was a bit like playing "beat the clock."

No alcohol to be sold after 9pm on Sunday.

I can't describe the emotion Dino and I felt as we arrived at the beer store at 9:05pm, seeing the workers doing their closing duties through the window, as one worker pointed at the very bold and prominently displayed sign that basically said that we were fucked by five minutes, and we needed to fuck off to someplace else.

PJ had beer for us. Not only did PJ have beer for us, she cooked burgers on the BBQ complete with fresh vegetables from her garden, and pickles she had grown and then canned herself.

We had some great meals on the trip, but this one was hands down the best. This one consisted of freshly grown food by our host and it was all prepared with the love only someone who knows the rigors of two-wheeled travel.

PJ wasn't trying to impress us with her hospitality, she has been us, and she knew that for the next seven days we would not feel anything approximating "home." For the most part, far from it.

We ate, we drank, we were merry, we got to take showers with soap and towels. Then, we went to bed on comfortable couches.

Smokers welcome!!

It was 2:30am when my alarm went off. At first, I wasn't sure I had slept at all, but I could tell I had, from the taste I had in my mouth.

As quietly as possible, we made our way to the kitchen, where I turned on the coffee maker PJ had set up the night before. We all had one cup of coffee, then pushed our bikes out of her driveway into the street, before starting them on a very cold, extremely early morning, in a small Colorado town.

We needed to be on the road by 3am if we were going to make it to the "Path of Totality." The Path of Totality was a (roughly) 50-mile wide path across the USA starting in Washington state, and ending in South Carolina where you could see the total eclipse for roughly 2 minutes 30 seconds at 11:30am, mountain time.

We had a 50-mile buffer zone, but The Professor, true to his name, had done his homework.

Every parking lot in every small town in the Path of Totality was charging $50.00 or more to see the eclipse from the convenience of their spot.

The spot The Professor picked out was on BLM (Bureau of Land Management) land. From our couches in Arizona, we were partial owners, and no one could tell us that we couldn't use it, nor could they charge us to use it. That's the beauty of public lands.

It was 3am, with almost no sleep, and the bitter cold, 80 miles of shivering, watching the deer's eyes light up alongside the road, while hoping none of them gets a wild hair up their ass and decides to jump out in our path.

80 miles of misery and questioning why I'm doing this.

As we pulled into Cheyenne, WY, you could see the traffic starting for the eclipse, as the free-flowing highway was starting to succumb to gridlock at 4:30am on a weekend, in a town not accustomed to any real traffic of any kind.

I had spent the last two months giving The Professor shit, believing there would be no traffic problems in Wyoming due to the eclipse. It had been a running joke at the TT on Tuesday nights, every variation of, "There are just not enough people as geeky as you to choke a freeway in existence."

Every one of those jokes were on my mind as we sat in traffic just outside of Cheyenne. I owed The Professor an apology, he had been right.

He wasn't going to get one.

But I owed him one.

The sun was coming up over bum-fuck-nowhere Wyoming, and it was a welcome sight.

It was still really cold for four guys from Phoenix, and I was ready to be warm at all cost.

You know that saying, "Careful what you wish for." The concept has bit every one of us in the ass at one time or another, and wishing to be warm, bit me in the ass, hard.

We were four or five miles south of Lusk, WY when all traffic in both directions stopped dead.

I got my wish. I was warm.

The midmorning sun was plenty warm, as I sat there with my air-cooled motorcycle getting hotter and hotter, as it idled away my fuel and my patience for 45 minutes.

45 minutes of shutting my motorcycle off periodically as we made a car-lengths distance every ten minutes or so.

After an hour, we made it to a long, sweeping corner that was going up a hill. For the first time, we could see just how bad the traffic jam really was, and there was no real end in sight.

Alongside the sweeping corner was a dirt road. We were in the middle of nowhere WY, so the maps on our phones were worthless, but after a short debate, I convinced the group to turn around in the emergency lane and follow me up the dirt road, my reasoning being, "Lost is better than sitting here."

Well, I guessed right.

The dirt road was hard on four bikes fully loaded for interstate travel, but we were moving, and we were soon to find out that we were moving in the right direction.

This was the only time on the trip I was to lead, and I led us about five miles up a hill to a "T" in the road, then turned left in the direction of what I assumed the position of the main road would be. In a couple of miles, we found ourselves in the center of the town of Lusk, WY, exactly where we wanted to be.

Not only had we found our way into the town we needed to be in, we were a couple of blocks past what had caused 15 miles worth of traffic jam.

What was it that had caused so many miles of backed up traffic?

The town's one-and-only traffic light.

Lusk WY, population 1,500 or less.

One of those towns that only has one gas station and two bars.

One of those small towns that don't really need a traffic light, but sometime in the 80's, the prom queen died in a drunk driving accident as she and her boyfriend left the prom, and now everyone trying to see the eclipse was going to pay because her boyfriend couldn't concentrate while getting a blowjob.

We were past the traffic stoppage and decided we should get some gas and take a little break.

This is where I found something that really should be on the signs for both Colorado and Wyoming. All over CO and WY are gas stations that have independent pizza ovens. I don't mean that they had good slices of pizza for a gas station, they had great slices of pizza for anywhere. I mean real baked deep-dish pies, for a couple of bucks.

Fed, rested, and a block or two north of the traffic bottleneck, we moved on.

Traffic moved at a relatively smooth pace for the next leg of the journey. There were still plenty of cars on the road, but people seemed to handle it better, as if they were over the initial shock of not being the only people traveling in this area to see the eclipse and resigned themselves to the fate of a slow and steady pace.

I am almost always running 20 to 40 mph over the speed limit, but I'll take five-under and moving, over stop-go, stop-go… any day of the week.

In the last town, before reaching our destination on BLM land, we stopped at a convenience store to gas up and for me to pick up some much-needed beer.

Normally, on a long ride like this, I have beer and will take the time to have a little drink along the way to smooth out some of the longer miles, but as I said, we failed to buy beer in Colorado the night before. I was seven hours into riding and had not had the chance to drink anything but coffee and water.

Once again, I was faced with culture shock in a country I have lived in my entire life.

The "Smoker Friendly"

That's right. The name of the gas station we stopped at was called "Smoker Friendly."

I've been smoking for almost 30 years. I clearly remember when you could smoke anywhere and everywhere. I remember when the host or hostess at every restaurant would ask, "Smoking or non-smoking?" and they didn't even screw their face up in a visage of disdain and distaste when you said, "Smoking."

I remember smoking inside, and honestly, after the last 15 years of standing in the rain, the cold, being looked at by passers-by as if you just whipped your dick out and shook it at them, it was glorious. I miss it.

Well, Wyoming is one of the last places left that you can still engage in the dreadfully evil activity of smoking indoors. Not only can you smoke indoors, they have a chain of convenience stores so dedicated to smoking they actually named the chain "Smoker Friendly."

I was so stoked on seeing the rows and rows of cigarettes and tobacco paraphernalia that I almost forgot I was trying my best to quit smoking after a recent diagnosis of Buerger's disease.

Oh yeah, stupid, fucking reality killing my good mood once again.

A field full of nerds...

What would have normally been a lonely patch of two-lane blacktop in the middle of nowhere, someplace where anyone would be speeding, due to the fact that you were not going to ever see people or anything else for that matter, was turned into a two-lane, 25 mile-per-hour zone. Every ditch alongside the road had cars, trucks, and campers parked nose to ass, with people setting up chairs and telescopes.

The BLM field we were going to was already full when we got there, with a neighboring rancher and his ranch hands trying to direct traffic.

This was another one of those times where being on a motorcycle was paying off in a big way. We were able to skirt the traffic jam and pull into a space right on the edge of the property that would not accommodate any other vehicle. Not only did we easily find parking, we were in a prime spot to view the event, and when the inevitable rush to leave after the event happened, we would be first in line.

After setting up, an easy task for four guys traveling light, I opened up a beer and started surveying the landscape.

Walking around, shooting pictures of the crowd, my first impression was of an open-air, Star Trek convention, where everyone forgot their Starfleet uniforms. Until, I saw several people in Starfleet uniforms.

The next thing I noticed was that I was the only person in a crowd of hundreds that was drinking. You would think that a professional drinker, such as myself, would not feel self-conscious drinking in a crowd of several hundred sober people, and three months ago, both of us would have been correct.

But after the stroke, my brain, and with it my confidence, were not what they once were.

I started feeling the first twinges of a panic attack, as I started to feel as though everyone was watching me, that everyone was judging, that any moment someone was going to call a cop to come fuck with me.

That's the insidiousness of what happened. I'm in the middle of nowhere, in a field, almost no one in a crowd of hundreds knows I was driving. It's perfectly legal for a grown man to drink beer on BLM land. The area I was in has almost no cops, any cop who would be nearby is working crowd control, and I'm literally covered in sweat thinking the cops are on their way.

I walked away from the line of campers, minivans, and cars. I crossed the lease road that bordered the BLM land and onto the rancher's property to sit alone on a large boulder that I thought was out of sight from anything and worked hard on calming the fuck down.

I was just getting my senses back when I heard a male voice say, "Hey man, you wanna get high?"

I turned back toward the BLM land to find two, young, bearded men in their early twenties walking up to me.

"I really wish I could man, I just had a medical issue a few months ago and I can't take the anxiety of smoking. I miss it though."

We talked a bit, they had spotted me out as one of their own, in a sea of people who were definitely not.

They gave me the abridged story of how they came to be here. They were from New Jersey, they were out of weed, they saw news of the eclipse on the news, Wyoming was close to Colorado, so this seemed like a great excuse to drive west in search of legal weed to bring back home, plus, see something cool in the process.

I don't remember their names. I'm sure they don't remember mine. But they were kindred spirits, and for a very brief time, my best friends in the world.

I was feeling more "myself" by the time the eclipse started. I was back at the bikes with the boys, I had drunk several beers, and was starting to feel all right.

I'm going to do a poor job of describing the eclipse in the Path of Totality. Unfortunately, it's one of the many things that you really needed to experience for yourself to really understand. But, I will try anyway, because if you paid money to read this, and I didn't... Well, that would be one hell of a dick move, now wouldn't it.

First, we saw the shadow. The Professor said that given how fast the shadow was moving, we probably wouldn't see it, but I swear I did.

Then, the moon started to fill up the sun. It was a sliver at first, much like how most of the country saw it. But that sliver was soon a circle, and soon the sun was gone.

As it happened, the first thing I noticed was that the temperature had dropped 15 to 20 degrees Fahrenheit.

Everyone around us went silent.

For 2 minutes and 30 seconds, it wasn't really night, it was some sort of deep twilight. It was not nighttime as so many portrayals of the total eclipse had described, it was some weird in-between stage I had never experienced before.

In the midst of totality, my mind raced.

I'm not a superstitious man. I don't believe in the supernatural. No gods hold any sway over me. I'm not even "spiritual" in any way, shape, or form.

But, for 2 minutes and 30 seconds, for the first time in my short life, I understood how people could be. Images of people, thousands of years ago, flooded into my head, what they must have been thinking as the sun suddenly went out.

You could see the sun's corona flaming outward from a perfectly black ring, and for the first time in as long as I could remember, I heard total silence as everyone there was in complete dumbfounded silence.

Slowly, the black disk moved off center and the real power of the sun started to shine past the edge of the disk.

As this happened, the silence was broken as thousands of people across the many miles in the Path of Totality all cheered at once.

Fat tires need love too...

Getting out of the field and back on to the main road was predictably a pain in the ass.

Even though we were in a great spot to make our egress, we had deep sand and confused bystanders, while on excessively loaded bikes to contend with. Honestly, I'm completely surprised that none of us dumped our bikes or got hit by a minivan while trying to get out.

Luckily for us, most of the traffic was heading south, while we were heading north. Not only were we heading north, but we were travelling the scenic route towards Devils Tower in Wyoming. Taking the scenic route was not only providing us a beautiful riding experience, it was dramatically cutting down the traffic flow.

I know it was scenic, but for the life of me, I don't remember most of the drive. I was right on the edge of being drunk, and the eclipse was such a profound experience, that it had completely occupied my thoughts for several hundred miles and two gas stops.

My next clear memory was of being afraid.

I grew up in northern Michigan. Other than the past 10 years, most of my motorcycle riding has been in northern Michigan.

I don't know what you know about Michigan, I'm guessing something about five big-assed lakes, and something derogatory about extremely well-fed mid-western girls?

Maybe about ass-deep snow?

Canadian accents?

Well, all of that is true, and if that's all you know about the state I was born and raised in, I won't fault you.

But what you may not know, is that Michigan is silly with white-tailed deer. Each year, more than 50,000 car accidents are caused by deer in Michigan. 50,000. And, that is only counting the people who report them.

Everyone I have ever known, in the 35 years I spent living in Michigan, has hit a deer, of all those people (quite literally everyone), not one of them reported the accident.

So, how does this little sub-story relate to my first memories after the eclipse?

The deer.

My first clear memory of this leg of the trip was seeing herds of mule deer alongside both sides of the road, as we entered the national park that houses Devils Tower.

A year ago, I would have made a mental note of the deer and kept an eye on them. Other than that, their presence wouldn't have caused me much concern.

But now, in this new reality I was fighting hard to escape, I was terrified.

I couldn't stop thinking about the last (and only time) I had hit a deer on a bike. I couldn't stop thinking about how much faster I was going compared to that time, how much bigger the bike I was riding back then was compared to the bike I was riding now, etc., etc....

We finally stopped at a runaway truck ramp on the side of the road overlooking Devils Tower. When I say overlooking Devils Tower, I mean from a distance. This was the first time you could actually see the monument.

This is where it got even weirder for me.

The Professor had stopped the group 10 or 12 miles from our destination, in a not very picturesque spot, then signaled for me to pull my bike up overlooking the tower but moved his bike away.

I parked, then walked up to his still running bike and motioned to him to say, "Huh?"

He said, "I thought you wanted a picture here."

I was confused. Between my deer terror, the events of the day, and really needing to land in our camping spot, I said nothing. I didn't pull my real camera out of its bag, I just snapped a pic with my phone. All the while, Dino and The German were looking at me with a very "WTF" look on their faces.

Then we moved on.

The KOA at the base of Devils Tower was a beautiful spot in the world, and The Professor had done a good job securing us the cutest cabin right in the shadow of the monument.

While The Professor was standing in line to check us in, Dino and I walked around the main entrance, store, gift shop, pool area, etc.… I spotted one of those coin operated mechanical horses I hadn't seen since I was a kid.

I was sipping on my flask of vodka, worn out from a very long day of riding, and needing some comic relief, I climbed on the mechanical horse with my best representation of a little kid on vacation in the west.

When it started to lurch back and forth, it was pretty funny. Then it started playing an "elevator music" version of the "William Tell Overture" (the Lone Ranger theme song). It got even funnier when it continued to lurch back and forth to the William Tell Overture for over three minutes, while a bus load of Asian tourists cheered and clapped. Well, it became so funny it was almost too much for me, as I laughed so hard, I cried, and almost fell off the fake horse made for children.

Once again, everything was going to be OK.

I wasn't going to drop dead right here, right now.

I was going to make my friends laugh again and again.

The sun was starting to go down when we finally got checked into the cabin. When I say cabin, I am describing it the way that I was picturing it on the long ride from Colorado.

Let me be clearer on the subject, the "cabin" was indeed in a log cabin, just in miniature. The interior size was roughly that of a large walk-in closet.

When you enter, there is about two feet of space that had pegs affixed to the walls for hanging coats, then on the left side were a set of bunkbeds, and on the right, a single regular bed, no wider than the bunkbeds.

It was enough for four close friends to bunk down for the night, it was even enough extra space for our gear, but just that much space, and no more.

It was so small that one bad fart was going to cause chaos, and we were three days into a road trip diet.

What the cabin site lacked in interior space, it more than made up for in exterior space and amenities.

Unlike the adjacent tent camping spaces, our space had a picnic table, a fire pit, and a shade tree. Amenities that would prove their worth, as we were to stay here two days, and be the longest place we would stay on the trip.

My bike, though not the most practical on a trip like this, with its suicide clutch and its stupidly low ground clearance, proved itself as the best wood hauling vehicle of the bunch.

With its 38-inch sissy bar, and custom-built luggage rack, it could easily mule four bundles of firewood from the main entrance to our cabin deep in the maze that was the KOA.

After getting wood from the store, and after a fair bit of drunken axe throwing at our shade tree, we started off to look for small sticks to start our fire.

We didn't make far from our campsite when a woman in her early 30's and a small pre-teen girl walked on to our campsite begging our attention.

The woman explained that her daughter (the little girl) had made a large quantity of fire starting aids with her Girl Scout troop, and given that this was their last day camping, they would like to give them to us.

Now, we are not the "dirty bikers" of film and TV, but anyone, three days on the road, and visibly drunk, looks a little rough.

We accepted the gift, even let the young girl get our fire going for us. We rewarded her and her family with dirty jokes, foul language, and Dino trying to light The German's farts. A pretty fair trade, all in all.

The next was to be a free day. The only free day in the trip. A day to fuck off and do nothing, relax, enjoy the scenery, etc....

Well, the boys had managed to get into my head. I had been nursing a fairly bald rear tire since leaving Phoenix. It was getting pretty bad, so bad that if a friend had posted the condition of his tire to social media, I would have tried to talk him into changing it.

But hey, we are all hypocrites in one way or another, and I really didn't think I had the money to replace the tire and take the trip.

You see, the bike I was riding is equipped with a 200mm wide tire. For you not familiar with the metric system, or motorcycle tire sizing (most of you by my estimation), my bike runs a ridiculously wide tire. So wide, that even though I live in the land of motorcycle shops on every corner, finding a tire this wide was a tall order, and an even more expensive order.

The width of the tire also makes it impossible for someone to change the tire without a shop with a specialized tire machine.

So, on our off day, our day to relax, I was on my phone hunting for a tire.

Being in the middle of nowhere in northern Wyoming, you would think finding a specialized motorcycle tire would be next to impossible, and it probably would have been, if not for the Sturgis Motorcycle Rally.

The Sturgis Motorcycle Rally is arguably the most famous motorcycle event on the planet. It is hosted in the small town of Sturgis, South Dakota, and has been going yearly in the first week of August, since 1938.

Well, it was the second week in August. Sturgis was over, but it being close meant there was a shop in the immediate area that might have what I need.

The first shop I called, audibly giggled under his breath when I told him what I was looking for.

The second shop, a shop in Spearfish, SD, about 70 miles from where we were camping, sounded doubtful, but the girl on the phone would look and see if they had one in their storage container behind the shop.

After what seemed like an hour, she returned to the phone.

"Sir?"

"Yes?"

"You are in luck, we have one."

Next, I proceeded to explain to her my situation, "Long trip"... "completely fucked"... "I only have $240."

After a long conversation between her and her manager, one that I was privy to, due to her not putting me on hold but simply laying the phone down, I got to hear him say, "Tell him to come in, it's not like we are going to sell that tire anytime soon."

Dino volunteered to ride out to Spearfish with me. He made the excuse that he wanted to buy a Sturgis Rally shirt for his son at a shop near the shop that was going to change my tire.

Dino is nothing, if not a good friend and stand-up guy. For of his east-coast Italian, and ex-military bravado, at times so hard on Irish ears, if he says he is going to be there for you, he is going to be there for you. Even if being there for you means sitting for hour after boring hour in a small motorcycle shop, while they took their time installing a tire they really weren't making money on.

The shop finally handed my bike back over to me with a receipt and a few choice words along the lines of, "Why would anyone run a suicide clutch and dirt bike tire in this day and age?"

Honestly, they could have called me Sally for I all I cared, they made the repair happen for the price I said I could afford.

Halfway back to the campsite, I started to notice a vibration in the bike that had not been there before changing the tire. Three-fourths to our destination, the vibration turned into a violent shaking.

Getting back to the campsite, we all looked the bike over. We couldn't find a thing wrong with her.

The next day we would be heading toward Sturgis, the Black Hills, Mount Rushmore, and Crazy Horse. To do so, we had to ride right past the shop that had worked on the bike, so instead of worrying about it, I made a cocktail and tried to enjoy the rest of my day in the shadow of Devils Tower.

The deer hunter...

The other guys took the tour. They went up to the base of the Tower and did the sightseeing thing.

I did not.

I had seen it years ago on a motorcycle trip, and as beautiful as it is, I realized that this was probably going to be the only time between now and the end of the trip that I could be alone.

From the outside, I may seem like I am never alone. Most of my social media posts feature friends and family having a very good time.

I do make plenty of time for friends and family and all of us having a good time, but the truth of the matter is that I am a bit of a hermit.

I cherish my time alone with my thoughts. So much so that I have structured my work life in such a way that most of the time I don't see or talk to anyone.

When I'm home, though my wife and kids know and are comfortable engaging with me, most of the time I'm hidden away in my own personal "fortress of solitude" that is my shop and office.

What did I do with my alone time?

My first thought was to jerk off. It had been a while, and it was going to be a few days longer.

But, days and days in close proximity to a bunch of guys, and complete lack of any kind of stimulating media, has the same effect as saltpeter.

Instead, I pocketed a couple of lenses and strapped my good camera on.

There were "no trespassing" signs every 30 feet along the fence line that bordered the campground. But, as most of you know, "no trespassing" signs or the ramifications for ignoring them, have had little to no effect on keeping me from doing what I wanted to do, or going where I wanted to go.

Right behind the fence was the Belle Fourche River. I breached the fence and started walking upstream.

Why did I walk upstream?

Because, I grew up trout fishing with my step-grandfather who had taught me that sound carries more easily downstream.

I walked about a mile when I saw a big doe, a big female mule deer. I watched her from the safety of about 300 yards for a while, all the while shooting pictures.

After several minutes, I was bored watching her and decided to test the skills I learned poaching deer in my youth and started to close the distance between her and me.

I was 30 yards or less when I stopped. I could have gotten closer, I was sure of that fact, but I saw the fawn (baby deer) hiding underneath a tree some 10 yards from its mother.

These deer were in no danger, my hunting days ended when I left the Midwest, and the only thing I was going to shoot were pictures, but I didn't want to disrupt the calm. These animals are always running for their lives, and I didn't want to give them a reason to run.

I shot several pictures of the fawn from 40 yards, and even more of the doe drinking from the river from 30 yards. Then, I belly-crawled backward away from them without them even knowing I was there.

The guys were sufficiently impressed with the pictures, even though I was showing them the pictures from the review window on the back of my camera. I know a couple of them were worried about leaving me alone. They were aware of the fact that I was still recovering, but these pictures helped set their minds at ease, as much as they did mine.

That night we had new neighbors. The girl scout and her family had moved on and their campsite had been taken over by a couple in a white one-ton van.

I was pretty drunk by the time they pulled into the spot, so drunk that I volunteered forcibly to help them back their van into their new camping spot.

They didn't call the cops at the drunk biker trying to direct traffic, fortunately. As they got out of the van, I could see they were one of "us."

Visible tattoos, a long beard on the man, bleached white hair on the female... This couple knew a Janes Addiction song that wasn't "Jane Says."

Later around the campfire, we would find out that they were astronomers here for the eclipse. When I say they were astronomers, I don't mean the multitude of amateur astronomers with their Walmart telescopes that we had seen all along the roadside. They were real, professional astronomers who work at a big-ass telescope in Houston, TX.

When this came to light, I literally saw The Professor's whole body shudder in involuntary, spontaneous orgasm.

I don't remember what we learned from our astronomer couple, in regard to astronomy, but I do remember that they had great senses of humor, and they had good cigars to share.

More good people we met, hung out with, and hope to see again one day.

Fat tires need love too... part two...

Morning was hard as usual, hungover, cold, and worrying about my bike shaking me from it.

We had a long, hard day ahead of us.

So many things to see in this area, and to make it worse, Dino had promised a friend of his that we would stay in his house in Colorado that night.

I think I have covered this in previous writings, but to recap, when you are on a road trip with multiple friends and multiple obstacles, don't make plans with your friends along the road.

You can't and won't keep your itinerary.

If you are in a car, van, bus... you might pull it off, on motorcycles? Nope, not possible.

You might be riding in a group, that group having basic shared goals, but you are still dealing with multiple singular entities.

You are also dealing with hundreds of miles, gas stops, places others in the group might want to spend more time than you can afford sightseeing.

So, take my advice. Don't plan to see friends along the route. If you happen to be in their town, and everyone wants to stop, that's great, but don't plan for it.

We made breakfast, packed our bikes, and hit the road.

To recap, if you have ever been on a trip with me, you know you never have to wait for me. When it's time to get moving, I move. I don't know exactly why or how this came to be. But making someone wait for me, is the most disrespectful thing I could do to a person.

It's as if I said, "You and your time mean nothing to me, and I will waste it as I see fit."

So, what happened next caused me intense anxiety.

We had to stop back by the shop that mounted my tire while they tried to figure out they fucked up. They had made Dino and I wait hours the first time we had been there, and I had no reason to believe we would not receive the same treatment this time, so I was really sweating it.

At first, the manager tried to blame my front tire, the dirt bike tire, the one they had not replaced.

I shut him down before he even finished his excuse, "I have 3,000 miles on that tire, 1,500 of those miles in the last four days, it was fine before I brought it in here!" getting pissed as I said it.

They had me unpack my bike and then hurriedly wheeled it into the shop while I stood watching.

It didn't take them long to figure out what they had done wrong. The guy who had originally done the tire change didn't see it, but the manager did as soon as he spun the wheel and touched the brake.

He looked at the tech who had performed the work and said, "You didn't put the brake shims back in."

The tech claimed he had, then the manager found my brake shims sitting next to the tire machine.

Next, I witnessed an ass-reaming of epic proportions, as the manager explained to the tech everything that can result in improperly shimming the brake, including the symptoms my bike was suffering.

Both men apologized, then went about the work of fixing the problem and throwing brand new brake pads in for free.

I repacked the bike, but the mental damage was done. I had held up the group on one of our longest days, and though none of them were giving me any shit for it, I could not stop thinking about it.

We made it deep into northern South Dakota with my bike handling as it should, finally.

We stopped in Rapid City, SD to get gas, and my already growing anxiety, got another kick in the balls.

I went to fuel up, and the credit card I use for fuel got declined at the pump. I walked into the store and tried to use it again, thinking it had to be some problem at the pump, and it was declined again.

This was a problem. First, there should have been at least $300 on that card. I hadn't used it for anything except gas, and I knew I had not fucked up and used it by accident, because I keep it in a separate compartment in my wallet. I literally only use it for gas for the bike.

I had cash, but not much, less than $100, not enough to cover the rest of this trip.

I used my debit card because my wife always keeps a few hundred in the bank for emergencies, fueled up, then called my wife.

Right about the time I called my wife, I got an email on my phone from my card company. They had shut my card down because they noticed multiple gas purchases outside the state I live in.

This would have been an easy problem to fix if I was an actual adult person who knew how to do actual adult things, but I'm not. I deal with this card exclusively through my laptop, not even through my main office computer, and had no idea what my passwords were.

My wife could tell I was in a bad way.

The entire time I was on this trip, I had been talking to her in the morning, then as soon as we set camp up at night. So, she was aware of what had been going on with the tire, and knowing me, and living through everything that had happened over the last three months, she knew I was on the edge of a full-blown meltdown.

She calmed me down by doing something she never does, telling me how much money we actually had.

My wife and I have been together for 24 years. She knows me better than any person alive or dead, and one thing she knows for sure, I'm shit with money.

I really am. I don't fully understand the concept, and I never will.

But, fortunately for both of us, she understands this and never really tells me how much money we have. What she does is she infers that we have next to none, so I keep making more and not spending.

Honestly, it's a good plan. If she didn't do this, I would spend it. All of it.

She told me to stop worrying and use our main credit card for gas and food, everything would be fine.

The growing anxiety, that started as soon as I woke up, let up a bit, just a bit.

Dead presidents and shitty friends...

I was riding through the famous Black Hills of South Dakota for the second time in my life.

The Black Hills are one of those places that every motorcyclist should visit at least once. Perfect, two-lane blacktop winding its way through picturesque mountain vistas covered in old-growth forest, with amazing granite outcroppings forcing their way out of the forest.

It isn't just beautiful, it's as if the designers of the road had tapped into the collective wishes of every motorcyclist who ever lived.

But thanks to my tire issues and needing to meet up with Dino's friend in Colorado, we had no time to explore and enjoy this incredible place.

We did stop at a couple of road side parks with partial views of Mount Rushmore and Crazy Horse, but only long enough to smoke a cigar and slam a beer, and that just isn't enough time to soak in the wonder and awe-inspiring magnitude of either monument.

There was a growing tension within the group, I felt like there was anyway. That's the problem when the anxiety starts to fully take over.

There may have been real resentment toward Dino and I for our parts in none of us getting to spend more time in this area. There may have been other resentments between other members of the group for reasons I was not aware of.

Or, and this is far more likely, there was no resentment and tension between anyone in the group, but my brain was jumping to conclusions that didn't exist solely based on my damaged perception of the entire situation.

I was constantly weighing all three of these possibilities in rapid, uncontrollable succession.

Months ago, before the stroke, I would have known. I would have addressed it with the group one way or another with a joke, or pep-talk, something.

But not now, not this time.

I wasn't even sure anything, outside my own head, was going on. I sure as fuck was not going to bring it up with my broken, disjointed stroke speech.

If I was right, if there was growing resentment within the group, I no longer had the ability to verbally defuse it.

If it was all in my head, it wouldn't be fair for me to make my comrades deal with my ever degrading mental and emotional state 1,500 miles from home.

Instead, I decided to keep my mouth shut and eat a Klonopin and wash it down with a big drink of vodka from my trusty flask.

I hadn't taken any anxiety medication so far on the trip.

I was trying my best not to and to ween myself off the stuff, given how addictive it is, and how it can flat out kill you when mixed with alcohol.

But, right this minute, I was glad I packed it. We were many miles south of the Black Hills, many miles south of twisting roads and natural beauty. We were deep into farmland and wide-open nothingness.

If not for the drugs, I would have continued to obsess about the dispositions of my riding companions to the point I would have had to stop and address it, or fully melt down into a non-functional, teary-eyed pile next to my bike.

Well, none of that happened thanks to the magic of Klonopin and alcohol. I ate away the miles of nothing, worrying about my heart stopping or falling asleep long enough to run me off the road, instead of worrying about the disposition of my friends.

That might sound almost hellish.

But it was better than how I was feeling before the drug.

We made it back into Wyoming, back to that same small town of Lusk where we had suffered gridlock just a few days and 700 miles ago.

I was still in rough shape. Rough enough that the guys were picking up on it, and Dino suggested that he and I walk to a local bar and have a quick beer.

I said quick beer, and I meant quick beer. It took longer for us to drink one PBR and take a selfie together, then it took for us to walk back from the bar.

I Don't remember the next 70 miles or so. Day drinking on anxiety drugs had done their work, leaving me with a very profound blank spot in my memory.

The next thing I remember was being back at the "Smoker Friendly" in who-the-fuck-knows-where Wyoming, drinking a parking lot beer.

I was in a decent mood again, except for dreading the long ride ahead. We had a few hundred miles to go before meeting up with Dino's friend in Colorado, and the sun was going down.

We mounted our bikes and The Professor started to lead us out of the parking lot when The German noticed The Professor's kickstand was still down.

On modern motorcycles, this would have not been a problem. Modern bikes have break away kickstands or kill-switches that shut the bike off if you put them in gear with the kickstand down.

But, The Professor was not riding a modern motorcycle. He was riding a 1980 Honda CB750, which was built with none of those modern safety measures. If he turned his bike to the left while riding, something he was about to do, as we merged onto the main road, his kickstand was going to jam into the ground like a pole-vaulter moving at 25 mph and weighing 700 pounds. You don't need to be a physicist to understand what was about to happen.

The German did the only thing he could do. He laid on his horn and yelled at the top of his lungs. The Professor, tired as we all were, heard the horn and looked back at us with a panicked look on his face and pinned his brakes as hard as he could at 5 mph, causing him and his bike, to abruptly come to a dead stop, then fall over.

It really wasn't a big deal. It didn't take long to get his bike back upright, but in the town of who-the-fuck-knows-where Wyoming, this was as much action as the townsfolk had seen all year.

Before we even got his bike back up on its wheels, townspeople were stopping their cars to help. Before we could push the bike back into the parking lot, we had attracted the attention of the one and only cop in town.

This wasn't really a problem, or it should not have been. The professor had not broken any laws, and this should have been a, "Yes sir, pushing it out of the street," type thing. But, The Professor was shaken from the incident, and for a short time, he was "stuck on stupid."

The cop had already assessed the situation and asked us if we could move the bike out of the road.

The Professor said yes and then proceeded to continue looking his bike over with a bewildered look on his face. He kept doing this for so long the cop started getting worried that The Professor really wasn't OK.

Trying to avoid the cop smelling my breath, as I explained that The Professor was tired from a long ride, and a little shaken but not hurt, I started pushing his bike into the parking lot myself.

The rest of the boys joined me as The Professor seemed to snap out of it and started talking to the cop in a normal fashion.

It took us a little while to make sure his old bike was not terminally damaged and get it started.

But, it did start and run properly.

It was going to live, and The Professor was going to live.

We had 70 miles to go before once again returning to Cheyenne, Wyoming, our next gas stop. 70 miles of straight, farm road in the dark. The only thing to see being the luminescent green eyes of deer alongside the road.

In Cheyenne, we stopped at a Denny's to eat.

As we were ordering, Dino got a text from his friend. His friend had seen the picture of Dino and me drinking a beer in Lusk, WY and was pissed off that we were drinking beer while making him wait.

Dino texted back an explanation of what was going on and received a reply, "My wife and I are going to bed, see you when we see you."

I literally laughed out loud. What a cunt. This guy is supposed to be a friend, and not only that, he is supposed to be a biker.

He knew how many miles we had done that day, and how many miles we still had to go to get to his house. None of that mattered to him.

It was 8:30pm and he expected us to be at his house by 7:00pm. We had tried our best. The road had not cooperated by 1.5 hours, and now his tender little feelings were hurt, leaving us with no place to stay.

Way to go dude. Our paths will eventually cross. When they do, I can't wait to publicly tell everyone what a little bitch you are.

Cancer and plan b...

Sitting there in Denny's, waiting for our food, and making fun of a cry baby cunt, I happened to check Facebook for the first time in a few days.

Honestly, I wish I hadn't.

My emotions were shredded from a very long day on the road, the tire fiasco, the bike drop, the cunt, etc.... But I did, and when I did, the very first post I saw was that a friend of mine had cancer.

When I say a friend of mine, I don't mean one of the people I currently hang out with daily anymore.

If it was, I would not have found out on Facebook. This was a person I was very close to at one time, and to this day, care very deeply for, even if I don't spend much time around him these days and may never again.

I wish that reading the news of his cancer, and my subsequent mini-meltdown, while waiting for my "moons-over-my-hammy," was solely based on worrying about my old friend, but it wasn't. Reading this news, in the most narcissistic way possible, was making me focus on my own medical problems.

As I said, Dino had noticed earlier in the day that I wasn't doing well and had started to manage me as best he could and was doing a pretty fair job of it.

Dino is a medical professional, as such, he has a multitude of professional contacts at his disposal.

Before I could even delve too deeply into my own problems, spurred on by the news of my friend's bad luck, Dino had texted a doctor he works with asking for an explanation of my friend's diagnosis and prognosis.

The doctor replied in short order. He explained that there are two forms of this cancer. Form one is pretty much a death sentence. Form two, the form my friend had, has a 98% survival rate.

I ate my dinner while trying my best to not think about the fact that fate had seemed to be catching up to me and my friends.

While I was fighting anxiety attacks, trying not to think about the inevitability of death, and being an altogether worthless, self-absorbed cunt, The Professor and The German were working on finding a place for us to camp in a metropolitan area.

Yes, I know that many of you, including me, would not consider Cheyenne, Wyoming as being a metropolitan area, but they have a Denny's, a college, and it's a motherfucker to find a place to tent camp in town, so I think it must qualify.

The German finally found a place just north of town, it was one of those places just outside of town that caters to retirees with RV's. These places litter the west. Almost every large to midsized town in the west has at least two.

The idea is, in the summertime, you and your elderly spouse live at the RV park in Wyoming, South Dakota, Idaho, etc.… In the winter, you move your RV to Arizona, Texas, New Mexico, Mexico, etc.…

Most of these places provide some sort of tent camping, but it's not their bread and butter, and the accommodations generally reflect that.

You are usually going to pop your tent right in front of the office or the bathrooms. You can't have a fire, you can't party, you better not make noise that might make the regular customers, people in their mid-70's, uncomfortable.

This place had all of those rules, we had to camp next to the community dumpster, but, our campsite had the softest grass and ground I had seen since leaving Northern Michigan a decade ago.

We set up camp in the dark, everyone made a halfhearted attempt at light partying and telling jokes, but we were all beat. I slammed 6 ounces of vodka and crawled into my tent and fell asleep without even needing to read a book to decompress.

I woke up in the morning feeling better than I had in a very long time. Sleeping on the soft ground, covered in soft grass, had done more than relax my beaten, tired body, it had relaxed my beaten, tired mind.

The fact that I had woken up in a particularly good mood, woken up completely, physically refreshed, does not mean that everyone had.

To this point, The Professor, every night before we went to bed, had lightly lectured us about the fact that we needed to get on the road earlier.

Honestly, it was good advice. But, given his increasing condescension, and the fact that most of our morning slowdowns had much to do with his fairly moderate OCD, there were moments of tension within the group.

I, for the most part, cut The Professor a lot of slack for his idiosyncrasies. I knew I was not the problem, my shit packs up in minutes, and he had done the work of planning this entire trip.

The German, on the other hand, woke up in a mood. I don't know why.

It might have been because of the fact his wife had been fighting cancer for the second time. Maybe he just didn't get enough sleep that night. Maybe it was because he is The Professor's best friend and felt like it was his duty to prove a point... I really don't know. I never asked, I only know what he did.

What did The German do?

He packed his bike in the most slow and meticulous way possible. We were there for at least an hour after breakfast, and every other bike was packed. He wasn't having problems, it was on purpose. He was trying to make a point to The Professor, and possibly Dino and I as well.

I don't know if his point was made with The Professor. I know it wasn't with me. I was perfectly happy drinking morning beers in the sun, laying on the soft grass. Take all the time you want, Bro. I'll be right here.

Our luck ran out...

We finally got on the road around 11am.

For the first half of the riding day, we were just going to plow down the freeway toward Denver, CO since "we" had wasted so much time getting ready in the morning.

I was fine with it, the freeway is easy, and there is no way to start zoning out on Colorado freeways now that their population seems to have tripled.

I know that Colorado is a beautiful place (or a small part of it is). I know it is the perfect mix of liberal public services vs personal freedoms, and of course, legal weed... But, holy shit, does it have traffic.

The last time I rode a motorcycle through Colorado was at least 25 years ago, and I know a lot changes in 25 years, but holy fuck!

Driving towards Denver now reminds me of driving west on interstate 10 just outside of L.A.

After fighting Denver traffic, we left the freeway and headed east on a beautiful piece of two-lane blacktop heading up and into the heart of the Rocky Mountains.

For the first hour or so, the riding was as beautiful as anything could be here on Earth. Mountain passes, valleys so deep you could not see the late-day sun, endless corners, endless trees and mountainous outcroppings, motorcycle heaven.

Then the worm turned, as it always must. So far on this trip we had experienced nothing but blue skies and comfortable temperatures.

That's not the norm on a motorcycle trip, usually within the first couple of days, the weather reminds you that you are stupid, and that you should be punished for your stupidity.

But no, this time the weather had waited until we were deep into the trip, and deep into the mountains.

When the rain started, we pulled over and parked in the parking lot of a small-town fire station to use our smart phones to look at the radar and to put on rain gear. Looking at the radar, and looking at the map, we realized we were fucked.

The road we were on, much like most mountain roads, had no detours that might lead us away from the storm front. We were going to be riding right though the worst of it, the heart of the storm.

The Professor, as I mentioned, has a bit of OCD. So much so, that he packed a back-up set of rain gear.

Well, I didn't pack anything in the way of rain gear. Honestly, in 25 years of riding, I never even considered rain gear.

I know the rest of the guys thought it was bullshit "tough guy" shit, and honestly, they were partially right.

I knew that you could buy motorcycle specific clothing designed for riding in the rain, but until very recently, every penny I could spare was spent on keeping the bike running, not making yourself comfortable in inclement weather.

Well, The Professor's OCD was my gain. As I said, he packed back-up rain gear, and though he is a bit OCD, he is not an asshole, quite the opposite.

He offered me his back-up gear.

At first, he seemed surprised that I had said yes, but I sure as shit said yes.

It was getting flat out nasty.

I won't act like the rain gear was comfortable, it surely wasn't. It was like wrapping myself in a loose condom. The noise coming off the suit as it flapped in the wind was deafening, it was hard to gauge my body position on the motorcycle, the flapping of the suit obstructed my vision...

But, I was way drier and warmer than I ever have been in a rainstorm at elevation.

Every other situation like this, and there have been many, I would try to curl up (as much as I could) into a tight ball, while trying to use the bike's front end as a shield for my body. The water would fly up from the tires soaking my legs all the way up to my crotch. I would ride the bike with only my right hand, using my left arm as a shield to aid in protecting the rest of my body from the force of the water hitting it at speed.

I didn't have to do any of that.

My feet got wet and cold.

My hands got wet and cold.

My face got wet and cold.

Other than that, I was fine.

After four hours of riding in the rain at 10,000+ feet, we made it to the campground. It was a beautiful place, even in the steady rain. High in the Rockies, with a mountain stream running right next to the campsites.

My phone is waterproof, so I volunteered to check the radar to find out how much longer we were going to be cold, wet, and miserable.

We were about to get lucky, it wasn't going to rain all night. According to my interpretation of the radar, something one generally gets very good at, if riding a motorcycle, I knew we had an hour to an hour and a half of rain left.

Everyone scrambled to set up their tents, I scrambled to make a fire. Everyone, to a man, seemed to think me nuts. I off loaded my gear into a wet pile and rode back down the muddy trail to the office to pick up four bundles of wood.

What I had noticed, that no one other than me picked up on, was that the firewood was neatly stacked under the eaves of a southeast facing building. The firewood was the least wet object in the entire campground.

Everyone was scrambling to set up their shelter, but I knew my shelter leaked.

My tent was wet. My sleeping bag was wet, my dry socks and my emergency socks were wet, and they were not going to dry until I made a fire and dried them out.

So as everyone else was setting up their tent and emergency awnings, while making snarky jokes and looking at me condescendingly, I was working hard on a fire.

I had no paper, I had no dry pine needles or leaves, all I had was a half-bottle of zippo fluid and an SOG "breaching tool."

The breaching tool isn't really an axe or a hatchet. It's a Vietnam era wartime tomahawk. But, good enough for soldiers in Vietnam, good enough for me.

I used my breaching tool to split the already split logs from the campground office into very small kindling and built a small pyramid of kindling over my driest t-shirt, poured all the contents of my bottle of zippo fluid over the entire lot, then lit the whole mess.

I had to babysit the small fire for at least 20 minutes, blowing and fanning the fire with one of my wet shirts, but finally, the flame took the wood and a real fire started to take shape.

The first thing I dried was the clothes on my body, then my bedding, then my spare clothes.

By 11pm, my tent was dry, set up, and containing my newly dried sleeping bag.

That night the temperature dipped down into the low 30's, but I was warm and dry because I sat in the rain making a fire.

That night we all drank heavily while I used my phone to play a mix of acid jazz and Liz Phair. I made the fire, I picked the music, as it should be.

OCDemetia and the Million Dollar Highway...

The group woke up at the usual time. That time being just after sun up. That's the thing about sleeping in a tent, no matter how drunk you got the night before, how little sleep you got, how badly you want to sleep in, as soon as the sun starts beating on the walls of your tent, it starts to get uncomfortably warm and humid and you will wake up. It's the ultimate alarm clock. No snooze button needed, just the inescapable humid funk of a hot tent.

Unlike the day before, the sun was shining bright, not a single cloud in the sky, but it wasn't warm.

We were "at elevation" and that means that even a beautifully, bright, sunny morning in August, at 7am we were going to have temperatures hovering around 37 degrees Fahrenheit.

I pulled the remaining firewood out from underneath the picnic table where I had stashed it the night before to keep it from getting wet, if more storms came in the night, and used the coals from last night's fire, still burning, to start a new fire.

Most of us, after making coffee over the campfire, started spreading our wet gear out on the grass in the open field next to our campsite so the sun could dry it out.

Unfortunately, The Professor, suffering from his OCD and terminal neatness, seemed to descend into a sort of madness born of wet gear and arrant mud.

While we all broke down our tents and spread our gear out on the unshaded ground, he made no effort to break down his tent. Instead, he kept his tent up and neatly hung up his wet gear from the mooring lines of his tent.

At first this wasn't a problem for any of us. We boiled our water to pour into our freeze-dried breakfasts, we had our fill of instant coffee, and we packed our bikes for the day ahead.

The Professor did all of those things, except he never packed his bike, he didn't even break down his tent. Instead, he just kept moving his gear around on the mooring lines of his tent and mumbling to himself.

Hours went by. Everyone's bikes were packed and had been for at least two hours. The Professor was still moving his gear around the mooring lines and folding, then refolding his clothes.

I went for several walks up and down the river, hiked the mountain twice, and even took a short nap on a picnic table in a bid to not let it bother me.

I was winning, for the most part, the war of not being bothered by The Professor's idiosyncrasies trapping him, and us along with him.

But I was not alone.

The other two men, The German and Dino, were struggling to remain calm. At 11:30am, five and a half hours from when we all woke up, Dino approached me with a plan.

We were to fake a trip to the office, tell The Professor that the manager had told us that if we didn't leave soon, we would be charged for another day of camping.

Well, Dino didn't even get his full plan out when a worker from the campground came barreling up the trail on a four-wheeler with a small trailer in tow.

Unlike us, she didn't give a shit about what the rain had done to The Professor and his OCD, she cared about cleaning up for the next ungrateful campers.

She yelled at us in an obviously practiced masculine voice, "Check out is at 10am. If you guys don't move yer shit, I'm charging you for another day and you need to move because this site is reserved for tonight."

Nothing we said to The Professor had lit a fire under his ass, but this big, flannel-clad lesbian woke him up. His camp was broken down, and his bike was packed in 20 minutes or less.

Our next destination would be the "Million Dollar Highway."

If you are unfamiliar with the Million Dollar Highway, located in western Colorado between the towns of Silverton and Ouray. It's 25 miles long and it will make you shit your pants. Narrow, two-lane blacktop, switchbacks cut into the side of a mountain with no guard rails, thousand-foot drops, and lots and lots of traffic.

I was really enjoying the first 10 or so miles of this incredible man-made wonder.

Then, just as I was really taking in the magnitude of such natural and unnatural beauty, that switch in my brain flipped. That switch that I never had before three months ago, that switch where my subconscious starts exploring all the possible horrors that could befall my friends and I on such a road, and started to force all of those possible scenarios into the forefront of my conscious mind.

I fought hard to force them out.

I started telling myself that it was all in my head (a true statement), that everything was going to be all right, that I can't let this brain damage rob me of this thing I love to do.

But, it was all for naught. The anxiety wheel had started spinning and it was gaining momentum with every mile.

I was trying my best to keep up with The Professor and The German, trying hard to focus on their tail lights instead of the tall cliff face to my left, and the 1000+ foot drop on my right, but I just couldn't focus on them as I fell farther and farther behind.

Finally, I hit a breaking point.

While trying to focus on them, I accidentally glanced to my left to the cliff face above. As I did, I watched something impossible. The cliff face started curling over from the top, bending, and curling down as if to swallow me up.

I knew it wasn't happening, I knew it wasn't real, I knew it was a product of fear chemicals flooding my damaged brain.

But knowing it, wasn't helping me not see it.

I slowed down to almost nothing, first gear, completely locked into what I was seeing and the sheer terror I was feeling.

Once again, it was Dino to the rescue.

Neither The Professor or The German could really see what was going on behind them, that's one of the many problems with riding overloaded motorcycles, but, as always, Dino was taking up the rear and he saw that I was in trouble.

He didn't try to pull up beside me and try to see if I was OK, he didn't try and talk me down, he down shifted, cracked the throttle, passed me, and pulled the leader over at the next pull-off available.

It took what seemed like hours to catch up to the group parked at the scenic overlook.

I pulled in, still in first gear, shut my bike off, then started crying. I stammered out what happened, but, by the looks on their faces, they knew what had happened.

As soon as I could collect myself, I chewed up a Klonopin, and smoked an entire cigarette, something I had not done since the stroke.

Within 15 minutes, I was completely fine, heavy duty tranquilizers are funny that way.

But that was the nefarious nature of these attacks. One minute you are enjoying yourself, the next minute you are having full-blown hallucinations, the next minute you are normal, all that's left of the experience being the memory and the shame you feel that it happened.

Back in the desert where I belong...

I don't really remember the rest of the ride out of the mountains. Klonopin and alcohol have that effect, as I have said.

My next memory was the desert. The beautiful desert with its dry air and heat. I remember being struck by the idea that I was still in Colorado, but now quite obviously in the desert southwest. I remember having a conversation with myself about how stupid it was that I was surprised by this fact, prompting an even longer conversation with myself, completely in my head about the history of western states' boundary lines.

Then, I realized that I was on a 500-pound Harley Davidson doing 85 mph with no safety gear on, while talking to myself, with no memory of the last 200 or so miles.

I pulled myself together just in time to pull into the KOA in Cortez, Colorado.

We unpacked our bikes, set up our tents, then Dino and I headed to the store to get beer and firewood, both being necessary for my continued convalescence.

That night I felt better than I had the entire trip. I cooked over a campfire while watching the sun go down over a beautiful desert vista. I drank many, many beers while sitting around the campfire telling jokes with my friends, and I slept in the warm, dry air.

The next morning, we woke as per usual as the sun came up. Everyone packed with purpose, no one seemed to be having attitude issues, or at least I was in such a good mood that I didn't notice anyone else's.

We were heading for Monument Valley near the Utah and Arizona border. A magically, beautiful place that I had only seen in pictures.

Riding through rural Utah, which would be the vast majority of Utah, is much like riding in rural Arizona. Long winding roads with spectacular views, and almost no people.

The desert southwest is nothing like how we were led to believe via the cartoons we grew up watching. Yes, there are coyotes, there are most definitely roadrunners. But, the desert is nowhere near the barren wasteland you may be picturing in your head. The desert is brown, the desert is green, the desert it full of trees, plants, and animals. What the desert doesn't have in any sort of large quantity, is people.

The few people you do find in the deep desert are hard, they are tough. They live a life where the elements are constantly trying to kill you via heat and dehydration, and there is almost no water anywhere.

The hardest, the toughest, live on the reservations. When I moved to this part of the world 10 years ago, I was told that people on the reservation hated white people, and for the most part, they probably do. I mean, who could fucking blame them.

But, the curtness I experienced at the gas station, deep into the reservation, deep in the desert, didn't strike me as hate for my race, it struck me as hard, cautious people, being cautious of strangers for all the reasons history and the landscape have taught them to be cautious.

Monument Valley is indescribably beautiful. Riding through it you could feel the millions of years it took to form such a place. It was the kind of beauty that could make me understand religion. If I were a god, I would have toiled millennia to create such a marvel, and the millions of years of toil and suffering would have been worth it.

Deep in Monument Valley we ate lunch. I don't remember the name of the place, but if you go there, it's the only restaurant overlooking the river, and it's the only restaurant, so I think I have narrowed it down as much as I can.

I fucked up.

I had a craving for a cheeseburger and fries, my normal mainstay in foreign restaurants. Up to this point on the trip, I had not eaten this meal once. I had been on a mission to eat as many local foods while eating out as possible. Well, I should have kept up that regiment.

I ordered a plain old cheeseburger and fries with American cheese, while The Professor and The German ordered this crazy cheeseburger meal served on Navajo frybread. Their meal was at least twice the size of mine, and from the small sample The Professor let me try, twice as tasty, at the same price.

We had made good time that day, well really, we made the same time we always did drifting between 75 and 85 mph, but we had gotten on the road much earlier than we had been, so it felt like we were making great time.

We made it to Tuba City, Arizona by 1pm, which was going to put us in Flagstaff, Arizona by 2:30pm at the latest.

I am mutinous scum...

The plan, as laid out by The Professor, was to camp in Flagstaff then ride home the next day.

Well, I'm a cunt.

We were going to arrive in Flagstaff mid-afternoon, which if we kept going, would put me back at my home by 6pm.

I'm all for adventure, I love camping with the boys, but I had been on the road for eight days. I really wanted a hot shower, I really wanted to see my kids, I really wanted to talk to my wife, and I desperately needed to get laid.

The idea of cleaning my road-weary body, then getting it dirty with my wife, was more than I could bear. In Tuba City, I made my intentions known to the group, and everyone but The Professor was of the same mind. We all missed our wives, we all knew the boring ride down the 17 (the freeway connecting Flagstaff and Phoenix), and we were all ready to be home.

The Professor made a halfhearted attempt to talk us out of it, to camp in Flagstaff, but our minds were made up, we were going home.

Just outside Tuba City, I noticed a strange vibration in the front end of my bike. We stopped in Camp Verde, AZ, some 50 miles from home, and I looked at the front tire. Every third nob, of my street legal dirt bike tire, had sheared off all the way to the steel belts, halfway around the tire.

Somewhere on the road, somewhere on the trip, I had hit something hard enough to knock my front wheel out of balance and it was only a matter of time for the tire to blow out and leave me stranded or worse.

But, it was going to make it 50 more miles to home. It's always going to make it 50 more miles to home.

Epilogue...

It's been almost a year since I had the stroke. I've relearned how to talk in a passable fashion. Hopefully, I have relearned how to write in a passable fashion.

It's been a long, hard road toward recovery, and it remains bumpy and full of potholes, at times.

But, then, as now, I'm going to make it.

If I can take a trip like this, so close to such a life altering event, I can do whatever it takes, no matter what it is.

Recognition and Honorable Mentions...

Mishka Shubaly: I was a fan, you turned me into a friend. Thank you for all of the comped shows and letting Mel see behind the curtain.

Dino, Christoph, and Steven: You guys held me up when I was sure I was going to fall down.

The fact that you never lost faith in my ability to keep going was where I drew the strength I needed to keep going.

My wife Mel, and my kids: I scared you, you never showed it. I will do better.

Jean Rusen: You never stopped sending me drunken text messages, and you never will.

My parents: You are the first email I send when life is getting to be too much. Thank you for always talking me down.

My brother Patrick: For knowing me so well that you are the only one I trust with all the ugliness.

And finally...

Jenna Hirt: My personal hero.

Made in the USA
San Bernardino, CA
27 August 2018